How to Analyse Bank Financial Statements

How to Analyse Bank Financial Statements

A concise practical guide for analysts and investors

Thomas Padberg

HARRIMAN HOUSE

HARRIMAN HOUSE LTD
18 College Street
Petersfield
Hampshire
GU31 4AD
GREAT BRITAIN
Tel: +44 (0)1730 233870
Email: enquiries@harriman-house.com
Website: www.harriman-house.com

First published in Great Britain in 2017
Copyright © Thomas Padberg

Print ISBN: 978-0-85719-518-0
eBook ISBN: 978-0-85719-519-7

British Library Cataloguing in Publication Data
A CIP catalogue record for this book can be obtained from the British Library.

For Rhea

Contents

Contents

About the author

Thomas Padberg, 41, is a German author. He completed his PhD on the subject of bank financial statement analysis and afterwards worked as a trainer and in-house consultant for many German banks within their specialist departments dedicated to this function. The German edition of his book – *Bankbilanzanalyse* – is now in its third edition and has become the standard reference work for the analysis of bank financial statements in Germany. You can contact the author at: tpadberg@trapeza.de

Acknowledgements

This book is the culmination of 20 years of research, accompanied by many changes in accounting rules and financial crises. My greatest debt is to my long-time co-author Thomas Werner, with whom many analysis ideas used in this book were developed.

Many other people played important roles in encouraging, challenging and critiquing me over the years. I would particularly like to thank my brothers Carsten and Christoph, Rolf Beike, Horst Gräfer, Thomas Kriete, Petra Oesterwinter, Bettina Schiller, Christiane Sorgenfrei, and Dagmar Tytko.

Last, but not least, I was very lucky to have a wonderful, insightful and extremely supportive editor, Craig Pearce. Craig's comments and suggestions have greatly improved this book, and his support for the project made the last year much more pleasant than it might have been without him.

Preface

What this book covers

This book is about how to analyse bank financial statements.

Bank financial statement analysis has to consider both banking supervision rules and banking accounting rules. These rules are not described in detail here, because this book is about the analysis and not about the rules. Therefore, it is expected that the reader has some background knowledge of these topics.

The data used in this book is mostly from the year 2014. It is already old data, but that does not impact the usefulness of the analysis methods shown in this book. The reader can use these methods to analyse any other bank financial statements.

Who this book is for

This book is written for all of those who are required to analyse banks professionally. The reader should have knowledge of both bank accounting and banking supervision.

How this book is structured

The book is divided into nine chapters. After an introduction in chapter 1, the specifics of bank financial statement analysis are covered in chapter 2. Here I answer the question of why a specific kind of analysis is needed for bank financial statements.

In chapter 3, I look at the accounting rules for banks which have direct implications on the analysis. Not all accounting rules will be mentioned, but only those that are used directly in the analysis.

Segment reporting is the topic of chapter 4. Here I show that segment reporting of banks is used very widely to interpret bank financial statements, but the data in this process can be manipulated very easily.

In chapter 5, I discuss widely used ratios for bank financial statement analysis. I show that most ratios have disadvantages which make them less useful for bank financial statement analysis. However, I show that there is one main ratio that can provide a quick view of the strength of a bank.

Chapter 6 is the most important chapter in the book. It looks at the analysis of the profit and loss accounts of banks.

The equity of banks is then analysed in chapter 7. In this area, banking supervision rules have a big implication on the analysis.

Chapter 8 looks at the stock analysis of banks. The connection between a number of ratios and bank stock prices is shown.

The book ends with chapter 9, which provides some important conclusions.

1. Introduction

In this book, the focus is on banks that are part of the Stoxx 600 Banks index. Other examples will be mentioned too, but mostly the focus is on comparable data from these banks. The constituents of the Stoxx 600 Banks are banks from member states of the European Union, which all use International Financial Reporting Standards (IFRS). This makes it easier to compare them directly.

This does not mean that non-IFRS banks cannot be analysed with the methods shown in this book. What it does mean is that for non-IFRS banks, accounting differences may exist and if this is the case these have to be analysed too.

Example

In Germany, under Handelsgesetzbuch, the German accounting law, it is allowed for banks to depreciate loans or securities up to only 4% of their nominal value. For this depreciation, there does not need to be a reason, such as the increased probability of non-repayment of a loan. Banks can just make the depreciation, without any economic reason. The legislator made this allowance to ensure that banks do not show losses in bad times, helping to avoid a bank run, because they can use these hidden reserves in such bad times.

Comparing German banks following Handelsgesetzbuch and banks following IFRS, these differences have to be eliminated.

Using IFRS does not mean that all parts of the balance sheet or the earnings statement are always comparable. National law can have an influence even on IFRS financial statements.

Example

Greece, Italy, Portugal and Spain give a special guarantee on the deferred tax assets of their banks, with the effect that the deferred tax assets can be used as equity. Most other countries in the EU do not grant this privilege.

In analysis, differences between national laws and how these impact the different numbers in the financial statements have to be recognised if possible.

In fact, the methods of bank analysis can be used on every bank in the world, but the accounting differences between national law and IFRS and their impact on the analysis have to be recognised in every case.

The following table shows the 45 banks of the Stoxx 600 Banks, their market capitalisations (market cap) at 2 October 2015 and their home countries. Their market capitalisation rank is also shown.

Name	Home country	Market cap (Bio. €)	Rank
Banca Carige	Italy	1.2	45
Banca Monte dei Paschi	Italy	4.8	36
Banco Bilbao Vizcaya Argentaria (BBVA)	Spain	46.3	8
Banco Comercial Portugues	Portugal	3.1	41
Banco de Sabadell	Spain	8.6	30
Banco Popolare	Italy	4.7	37
Banco Popular	Spain	7.0	33
Banco Santander	Spain	65.8	3

Name	Home country	Market cap (Bio. €)	Rank
Bank of Ireland	Ireland	11.2	27
Bankia	Spain	13.3	25
Bankinter	Spain	5.9	34
Barclays	UK	55.4	6
Banca Popolare di Sondrio	Italy	1.8	43
Banca Popolare dell'Emilia Romagna	Italy	3.6	39
BNP Paribas	France	64.7	4
Caixabank	Spain	20.1	22
Commerzbank	Germany	11.8	26
Credit Suisse	Switzerland	34.5	10
Crédit Agricole	France	26.6	16
Danske Bank	Denmark	27.2	15
Deutsche Bank	Germany	32.8	12
DNB	Norway	19.3	23
Erste Group Bank	Austria	11.0	28
HSBC	UK	134.3	1
Intesa Sanpaolo	Italy	48.8	7
Julius Bär	Switzerland	9.4	29
Jyske Bank	Denmark	4.7	37
KBC	Belgium	23.5	18
Komercni Banka	Czech Rep.	7.5	31
Lloyds	UK	73.9	2
Mediobanca	Italy	7.5	31
National Bank of Greece	Greece	1.3	44
Natixis	France	15.5	24

Name	Home country	Market cap (Bio. €)	Rank
Nordea Bank	Sweden	41.4	9
Raiffeisen	Austria	3.4	40
Royal Bank of Scotland	UK	27.6	14
SEB	Sweden	20.9	21
Société Générale	France	31.9	13
Standard Chartered	UK	23.0	19
Svenska Handelsbanken	Sweden	23.9	17
Swedbank	Sweden	22.5	20
Sydbank	Denmark	2.5	42
UBS	Switzerland	61.0	5
UniCredit	Italy	33.2	11
UBI Unione di Banche	Italy	5.8	35

Nine of the 45 banks come from Italy, but simple numbers like this do not show the strength of a banking system. All Italian banks in the Stoxx 600 Banks together have a lower market capitalisation than HSBC alone.

In addition, the size of an economy is no indicator for the well-being of its banking system. Germany is the largest economy in Europe, but its banks are ranked 12th and 26th. Spain, with a suffering economy, has seven banks out of the 45, with Banco Santander ranked third. The best banks, as ranked by market capitalisation, come from the United Kingdom, with HSBC far above all others.

A weak home economy can weaken its banks if they are concentrated only within that country. This is the case for the Italian banks and most of the Spanish banks (except Santander and BBVA). However, with the right strategy, even with a tumbling home economy, a bank can not only survive but even come out of an economic crisis strengthened. The correct strategy depends on the circumstances, the home economy and so on. An example of a bank that came through the world financial crisis strongly is the Spanish Banco Santander, which even made acquisitions at that time and diversified its risk through different countries.

Strategy is not the focus of this book, but to a degree a bank's strategy has an influence on the analysis.

Many countries in the world use IFRS. In the European Union it has to be used by all publically listed companies; in Chile, Honduras and Kenya it has to be used by all companies; in Abu Dhabi, Belarus, Iraq, Jordan, Kazakhstan, Latvia and Liberia all banks have to use it.

However, some countries – such as Indonesia – do not allow banks to use IFRS, but exchange their national law step-by-step with IFRS without accepting all standards or every standard fully. Some differences in accounting may still exist, but nevertheless banks from most countries make their financial statements according to IFRS (www.iasplus.com/en).

In fact, banks are much more comparable worldwide than non-banks, since many countries specifically demand that their banks use IFRS. Therefore, the methods shown in this book can be used to analyse banks around the world and not just European banks.

Note

European banks are used as an example in this book, but the analysis methods can mostly be used for banks worldwide.

2. Specifics of Bank Financial Statement Analysis

Liabilities and equity

Banks differ in many ways from non-banks. First, we have to mention the method of business. Liabilities in non-banks have the task of financing the assets. A company would not increase its liabilities without knowing what to do with the money on the assets side, for example to finance a new factory.

For banks, liabilities are a normal part of their business. If a bank can find liabilities for which it has to pay less interest than it gets risk-free for assets, e.g. AAA-bonds, it will increase its liabilities as much as possible. So, in fact, banks tend to raise their total assets/total liabilities as much as possible.

On the other hand, for non-banks, high total assets are not a sign of a healthy company but more a sign of mismanagement. A non-bank can work with very few assets when all long-term assets are leased (operating leasing). For a bank, the total assets/total liabilities are a sign of strength.

Another specialty of banks is equity. Non-banks can operate with negative equity, but banks cannot. Banking supervision in many countries in the world follows the rules of the Basel Committee on Banking Supervision. A list of members represented on the Basel Committee on Banking Supervision can be found on the Bank for International Settlements (BIS) website (www.bis.org/bcbs/membership.htm). The rules of banking supervision demand that banks have a minimum level of equity in relation to their risks, measured by so-called risk-weighted assets (RWA). If a bank fails to meet the rules of banking supervision, it can be closed down. Therefore, it is the main task for bank management to always conform to all rules of banking supervision. Independent from internal risk measurement or any other method for measuring the risks of a bank, the banking supervision regulation rules on equity are a limiting factor for bank business.

Predictability of future earnings

In terms of analysis, a big difference between banks and non-banks is the predictability of future earnings.

Example

Let's take, for example, a car manufacturer. The car manufacturer last year made revenues of €500 Mio. Can it repeat these revenues? Maybe it can, maybe it cannot. What is relatively certain is that the revenues will not be made with the same customers again!

For a bank, depending on their maturity structure, many or most earnings and expenses for the next year and even years after are safe. We do not need to discuss the attractiveness of the product portfolio, new emission standards or whatever else, because for the bank the transactions of the past will also make a profit in the future. This makes bank financial statement analysis somewhat boring, because we do not need to look at new cars, the attractiveness of brands and so on, year by year.

In this sense, the analysis of banks and non-banks is different. For a non-bank, we can hope that the earnings from last year will be repeated next year. For a bank, we mostly know which earnings and expenses will be repeated in the next year and partly also in the years after.

While the ability to repeat earnings is much less of a problem for banks than for non-banks, we can investigate the risks of a bank much more than for a non-bank. For example, an economic crisis has influence in several ways on a bank:

- Customers cannot pay their credits, so the predicted earnings go down.

- Customers do not ask for new loans, so the predicted new business does not arrive.

- The provisions income goes down because customers do not trade as much as before on the stock exchange, and do not require the kind of services which lead to provisions income.

- The trading income will go down because fewer customers ask for derivative products.

Evaluating risks

Bank financial statement analysis also has the task of evaluating the risks of a bank as much as possible from its financial statement. Risks we can uncover from the financial statement of a bank are as follows:

- The volatility of trade income shows the risk of changing earnings.

- Volatile trade income combined with sometimes negative trade income can even show the risk of bankruptcy.

- The volatility of provisions income is an indicator for the risk of changing earnings in this area.

- A low interest margin after provisions shows the risk of underpricing risks, so that in the event of an economic crisis this margin will become negative, which can lead to bankruptcy.

- Low profit combined with low capital can lead to bankruptcy in an economic crisis.

- A high interest margin due to high maturity transformation can lead to a high negative interest margin when there is an inverted yield.

- Additionally, a high maturity transformation can lead to bankruptcy if bank debt has to be repaid and no refinancing can be found.

Sometimes it is very hard to identify these kinds of risks from the financial statements. We can identify one or many of these risks mentioned for the bank failures in the financial crisis of 2007-2008. High maturity transformation for Dexia or Depfa, too little interest margin for many German *Landesbanken*, and so on.

We cannot identify which bank(s) will fail next. The failure of a bank not only depends on the key financial figures but also on political factors, the ability to sell the bank partly or in whole, the general economic situation, and so on.

What we can identify are banks which have insufficient earnings compared with the risks they take. These kind of banks have the highest risk of getting into an unprofitable situation if the economy suffers, the stock exchange crashes, or something similar. To make business with those kind of banks has a higher risk than with the stable, low-risk banks.

In many cases, other reasons are more important than the key financial figures in the failure of banks. It is an additional task in analysing the risk of a bank's failure to review these kinds of topics. In this book, the focus is limited to the financial aspects and I do not consider political reasons or any other possible causes of bank failure.

3. Accounting Rules for Banks

In this chapter I look at the accounting rules for banks which have direct implications for bank analysis. I have deliberately not included all accounting rules because this is a book for financial statement analysis and not for accounting, but sometimes it is very helpful to look at the accounting notes to see how problems were solved by a bank. This can help the analyst understand if the bank used accounting rules to show higher profits and equity.

The main accounting rules covered in this chapter are:

1. Goodwill

2. Provisions

3. Deferred taxes

4. Level 3 assets

It is not correct to say that a bank which does not do anything in these areas is healthy and has no problems. However, for a bank which uses these rules to look better in financial statements, it is necessary to look much more closely than with a bank which shows no problems in these areas.

3.1 Goodwill

Goodwill is not an identifiable asset like a financial instrument or even a brand name; it is intangible. It is comprised mostly of synergy effects and so on. The intangible assets of a bank normally consist of:

- In-house developed software
- Customer relationships
- Goodwill
- Purchased brand names
- Other similar aspects

Banks normally have their own in-house developed software. This is normally the only part of the intangible assets which is developed in-house. All other parts come from acquisitions.

The value of in-house developed software in the balance sheet is highly connected to the total assets – the bigger the bank, the higher the value of the in-house-developed software. For example, HSBC has a net carrying amount of 2,127 Mio. US-$, Deutsche Bank of 2,466 Mio. € and Handelsbanken of 1,152 Mio. SEK (€122 Mio. on 31/12/2014).

As mentioned, apart from software, goodwill usually originates from acquisitions of other banks. We can say that the more acquisitions a bank has made in the past, the higher value the intangible assets will have. There are banks with very few acquisitions – like Jyske Bank – that have very low amounts of intangible assets, but also banks like Deutsche Bank, HSBC or Royal Bank of Scotland, which grew because of acquisitions. These banks have high amounts of the intangible assets because of these acquisitions.

In the case of an acquisition, the buyer has to value all assets and liabilities of the acquired bank at their fair value. While self-made brand names, customer relationships and so on are not allowed to be activated, in the case of an acquisition these positions have to be activated at their fair value. We could think about how to value a brand name. For example, the brand value of Coca-Cola has been measured in the past with values between $0.2bn and $64bn.[1] So if we buy Coca-Cola now, we can activate 200 Mio. US-$ or 64,000 Mio. US-$. Even without discussing this any further, we can see that brand valuation is a highly debatable topic. These kind of values are used when a bank acquires another bank!

Example

When Commerzbank bought Dresdner Bank, it mainly discontinued the use of the brand 'Dresdner Bank'. Only its branch in Dresden still uses this name. Therefore, Commerzbank cannot use the brand name 'Dresdner Bank' in its intangible assets anymore.

After all identifiable assets and liabilities have been valued, the difference between assets and liabilities can be calculated. This is the equity amount the bank acquires. The amount paid to acquire the bank will normally be different from this. If the paid amount is higher than the equity acquired, the difference between the paid amount and equity will be activated as goodwill. If the paid amount is lower than the equity acquired the difference will be used as earnings in the income statement immediately.

During the financial crisis many banks lost market capitalisation and in some cases stock exchange share prices were lower than the equity per share figure on the balance sheet. Banks which made acquisitions in the financial crisis sometimes paid less than the equity they acquired, which directly increased their earnings.

Example

In 2014, German Aareal Bank bought German Corealcredit Bank for 346 Mio. €. The equity acquired was 500 Mio. €. The difference of 154 Mio. € Aareal Bank used directly in its earnings. The profit for the period reached 335 Mio. € compared to 136 Mio. € the year before. The increase of 199 Mio. € consists of 154 Mio. € from

---

1. Bekmeier-Feuerhahn: *Marktorientierte Markenbewertung.* 1998, S. 62.

purchase earnings of Corealcredit Bank and only 45 Mio. € from operating earnings.

Note

If a bank acquired other banks in the analysed period, we always have to look for the effect of the acquisition on the earnings!

For the analysis, what is most important is not the first valuation when another bank is acquired, but the valuation models used in the following periods.

Example

Commerzbank acquired Dresdner Bank in 2009. In the notes, it mentioned: "This goodwill is based in particular on the utilization of staff and bank expertise, access to new potential future markets and expected cost savings from economies of scale." (Commerzbank, Annual report 2009, p. 202).

Goodwill cannot be valued itself. Because of this, IFRS forces companies to build cash-generating units (CGU), which are valued together. Without going too deep into the accounting rules, we can just say this: goodwill impairment has to be made if the value of the CGU is lower than its book value (so-called impairment testing). The value is normally identified by the present value of the future cash flows of the CGU.

For calculating the value of a CGU, three steps have to be followed:

1. Calculate the future cash flows.

2. Calculate the discount rates.

3. Calculate the present value by using 1 and 2.

Naturally, banks do not publish their expected future cash flows, but they have to publish the discount rates they use. Discount rates reflect the cost of capital a CGU uses. Mostly banks refer here to the capital asset pricing model (CAPM), from which they calculate their discount rates. The lower the discount rate, the lower the estimated risk for this CGU!

To get a feeling for discount rates, the published discount rates from a number of banks are shown in the tables below.

HSBC: Discount rates 2014 (Annual report 2014, p. 409)

	Discount rate 2014	Discount rate 2013
Retail Banking and Wealth Management – Europe	9.1%	8.0%
Commercial Banking – Europe	10.1%	10.0%
Global Private Banking – Europe	7.1%	7.3%
Global Banking and Markets – Europe	11.0%	9.9%
Retail Banking and Wealth Management – Latin America	12.8%	11.2%

HSBC uses a combined regional and business approach in its segment reporting. The highest risk is in the regional market of Latin America. In Europe, Global Private Banking has the lowest risk, followed by Retail Banking and Wealth Management and Commercial Banking.

Crédit Agricole: Discount rates 2014 (Annual report, p. 232)

	Discount rate 2014
French retail banking	8.3%
International retail banking	10.0–16.9%
Specialised financial services	8.3–8.7%
Savings management and Insurance	8.3–9.2%
Corporate and investment banking	10.0%

Crédit Agricole has the joint-lowest risk in French retail banking, while its international retail banking has a discount rate of up to 16.9%.

Société Générale: Discount rates 2014 (Annual report, p. 86)

	Discount rate 2014
French retail banking	8%
International Retail Banking and Financial Services	
Retail banking and Consumer finance	10.2–13.9%
Insurance	9.0%
Professional Equipment Financing and Auto Leasing Financial Services	9.7%
Global Banking and Investor Solutions	
Corporate and Investment Banking	11.0%
Private Banking and Securities Services	9.0–9.2%

Société Générale has – along with Crédit Agricole – the joint-lowest risk in French retail banking, while its international retail banking has a discount rate of up to 13.9%.

Commerzbank: Discount rates 2014 (Annual report, p. 175)

	Discount rate 2014
Private Customers	11.7%
Mittelstandsbank	12.1%
Corporates & Markets	12.3%
Central & Eastern Europe	9.4%

Commerzbank uses a discount rate of 11.7% in the CGU Private Customers. Compared to the French banks and French retail banking, the discount rate for the German market is much higher.

What can this data tell us?

First, most banks are very reluctant to give full information. Commerzbank gives the information that the discount rates are before tax (Annual report, p. 175), while we cannot find any comparable information for the other banks mentioned above. If Commerzbank's discount rate is the only one given before tax and all others are given after tax, we cannot compare them.

The data in the tables gives the impression that Commerzbank, in general, uses higher discount rates than the other banks. But even Commerzbank uses for Central & Eastern Europe a very low discount rate compared to the other three discount rates it uses. This implies that Central & Eastern Europe is less risky than, for example, Germany. On the other hand, the effect of the lower discount rate is not that great because the goodwill of the CGU Central & Eastern Europe is only €226 Mio. compared to €1,079 Mio. for Private Customers (Annual report 2014, p. 211).

Second, we always have to include a second rate in this analysis. To understand this part, we have to go back to the calculation of the impairment testing. We noted that the impairment testing has three steps. The first step is the estimation of the future cash flows. Normally banks (and all other companies too) only estimate for a number of future years (five years usually) and calculate for the time after with a constant or a constantly growing cash flow. The present value of constant future cash flows is calculated as follows:

constant future cash flow / discount rate

Including a constant growth rate for the cash flow, the present value is calculated as follows:

constant future cash flow / (discount rate – constant growth rate)

In fact, the constant growth rate is subtracted from the discount rate. The higher the growth rate, the lower the denominator and therefore the higher the present value.

To calculate a present value with which a bank must not make an impairment, there are two different methods:

1. Choose a low discount rate, or

2. Choose a high discount rate with a high constant growth rate!

Naturally, the constant growth rate cannot just be as high as a company wishes it to be. The natural border is the estimated world economic growth rate. If a company always grew faster than the world economy, it would be mathematically bigger than the world economy in the infinity. This is not possible.

The average world economic growth over the last ten years was 3.9%.

In the next step, the tables below show the growth rates used by the banks mentioned above.

HSBC: Growth rate 2014 (Annual report 2014, p. 409)

	Growth rate 2014	Growth rate 2013
Retail Banking and Wealth Management – Europe	4.5%	3.9%
Commercial Banking – Europe	4.2%	3.4%
Global Private Banking – Europe	3.4%	3.0%
Global Banking and Markets – Europe	4.2%	3.7%
Retail Banking and Wealth Management – Latin America	7.9%	8.6%

All growth rates but Global Private Banking – Europe are higher than the world economic growth rate of the last ten years. This is an indication that HSBC uses the discount rates combined with the growth rates to give a higher value for their goodwill. Let us look at the discount rate minus growth rate for HSBC for 2014:

	Discount rate 2014	Growth rate 2014	Discount rate minus growth rate 2014
Retail Banking and Wealth Management – Europe	9.1%	4.5%	4.6%
Commercial Banking – Europe	10.1%	4.2%	5.9%
Global Private Banking – Europe	7.1%	3.4%	3.7%
Global Banking and Markets – Europe	11.0%	4.2%	6.8%
Retail Banking and Wealth Management – Latin America	12.8%	7.9%	4.9%

Now we can see that for all CGUs the discount rate minus the growth rate is very low. Global Private Banking – Europe has only 3.7%. Latin America is less than 5%. Consider the high inflation rates there! The risk-free interest rate in these regions is only a little bit lower than the discount rates the bank uses. Would you invest in these segments for an expected return just a bit higher than the risk-free interest rate? I would imagine not.

Crédit Agricole: Growth rates 2014 (Annual report, p. 232)

	Growth rate 2014
French retail banking	2.0%
International retail banking	2.0–5.0%
Specialised financial services	2.0%
Savings management and Insurance	2.0%
Corporate and investment banking	2.0%

Crédit Agricole uses much lower growth rates than HSBC. Only for international retail banking is the higher value of 5.0% above the world economic growth rate. On first view, Crédit Agricole is much more conservative in accounting than HSBC because the growth rates are so much lower.

As for HSBC, we next calculate the discount rates minus growth rates for 2014.

Crédit Agricole: Discount rates minus growth rates 2014 (Annual report, p. 232)

	Discount rate 2014	Growth rate 2014	Discount rate minus growth rate 2014
French retail banking	8.3%	2.0%	6.3%
International retail banking	10.0–16.9%	2.0–5.0%	8–11.9%
Specialised financial services	8.3–8.7%	2.0%	6.3–6.7%
Savings management and Insurance	8.3–9.2%	2.0%	6.3–7.2%
Corporate and investment banking	10.0%	2.0%	8.0%

The discount rate minus growth rate of Crédit Agricole for all CGUs is much higher than for HSBC. Again, this suggests Crédit Agricole is much more conservative than HSBC.

Société Générale: Growth rates 2014 (Annual report, p. 86)

	Growth rate 2014
French retail banking	2%
International Retail Banking and Financial Services	
Retail banking and Consumer finance	3–3.5%
Insurance	2.5%
Professional Equipment Financing and Auto Leasing Financial Services	2.0%
Global Banking and Investor Solutions	
Corporate and Investment Banking	2.0%
Private Banking and Securities Services	2.0%

Like Crédit Agricole, Société Générale uses much lower growth rates than HSBC. Again, we next calculate the discount rate minus growth rate.

Société Générale: Discount rates minus growth rates 2014 (Annual report, p. 86)

	Discount rate 2014	Growth rate 2014	Discount rate minus growth rate 2014
French retail banking	8%	2%	6%
International Retail Banking and Financial Services			
Retail banking and Consumer finance	10.2–13.9%	3–3.5%	7.2–10.4%
Insurance	9.0%	2.5%	6.5%
Professional Equipment Financing and Auto Leasing Financial Services	9.7%	2.0%	7.7%

	Discount rate 2014	Growth rate 2014	Discount rate minus growth rate 2014
Global Banking and Investor Solutions			
Corporate and Investment Banking	11.0%	2.0%	9.0%
Private Banking and Securities Services	9.0–9.2%	2.0%	7.0–7.2%

As for Crédit Agricole, the discount rate minus growth rate for Société Générale is much higher than for HSBC, so the bank uses the accounting rules much more conservatively.

Commerzbank: Growth rates 2014 (Annual report, p. 173)

	Growth rates 2014
Private Customers	1.5%
Mittelstandsbank	1.5%
Corporates & Markets	1.5%
Central & Eastern Europe	1.75%

Of all banks mentioned here, Commerzbank uses the lowest growth rates. Next we calculate Commerzbank's discount rates minus growth rates.

Commerzbank: Discount rates minus growth rates 2014 (Annual report, pp. 173, 175)

	Discount rate 2014	Growth rates 2014	Discount rate minus growth rate 2014
Private Customers	11.7%	1.5%	10.2%
Mittelstandsbank	12.1%	1.5%	10.6%
Corporates & Markets	12.3%	1.5%	10.8%
Central & Eastern Europe	9.4%	1.75%	7.65%

Commerzbank's discount rates minus growth rates are the highest of all the banks mentioned here. Central & Eastern Europe again has the lowest value of Commerzbank's CGUs.

The values investigated here are indications of higher risks in goodwill but not proof. To get a better feeling about the risk in this position, we have to include the value of goodwill in the analysis too.

This is done for the four example banks in the following tables.

HSBC: Discount rate minus growth rate and goodwill 2014

	Discount rate minus growth rate 2014	Goodwill ($m)
Retail Banking and Wealth Management – Europe	4.6%	4,298
Commercial Banking – Europe	5.9%	3,214
Global Private Banking – Europe	3.7%	3,808
Global Banking and Markets – Europe	6.8%	3,296
Retail Banking and Wealth Management – Latin America	4.9%	1,762
Total goodwill		16,378

	Discount rate minus growth rate 2014	Goodwill ($m)
Equity		199,978
Profit for the year		14,705

HSBC has in total $16,378 Mio. of goodwill. Compared to the equity, even a full impairment would not be a big problem. From the point of view of the shareholders, it would be a bit more than a one-year profit, so for the share price this could be a problem.

Crédit Agricole: Discount rate minus growth rate and goodwill 2014

	Discount rate minus growth rate 2014	Goodwill ($m)
French retail banking	6.3%	5,559
International retail banking	8–11.9%	2,119
Specialised financial services	6.3–6.7%	1,024
Savings management and Insurance	6.3–7.2%	4,716
Corporate and investment banking	8.0%	487
Total goodwill		13,976
Equity		91,643
Profit for the year		5,279

We can see that Crédit Agricole has a much higher risk in goodwill than HSBC. Compared to the equity, goodwill has only a percentage of 15%. Compared to the profit, it is nearly three times higher. A full impairment would be a big, big problem for Crédit Agricole.

Société Générale: Discount rate minus growth rate and goodwill 2014

	Discount rate minus growth rate 2014	Goodwill ($m)
French retail banking	6%	798
International Retail Banking and Financial Services		2,686
Retail banking and Consumer finance	7.2–10.4%	
Insurance	6.5%	
Professional Equipment Financing and Auto Leasing Financial Services	7.7%	
Global Banking and Investor Solutions		847
Corporate and Investment Banking	9.0%	
Private Banking and Securities Services	7.0–7.2%	
Total goodwill		4,331
Equity		58,813
Profit for the year		2,991

Société Générale has no problems with goodwill relating to equity, but if a full impairment was required, it would cost nearly 1.5 years of profit, with perhaps a big effect on the share price.

Commerzbank: Discount rate minus growth rate and goodwill 2014

	Discount rate minus growth rate 2014	Goodwill ($m)
Private Customers	10.2%	1,079
Mittelstandsbank	10.6%	633

	Discount rate minus growth rate 2014	Goodwill ($m)
Corporates & Markets	10.8%	138
Central & Eastern Europe	7.65%	226
Total goodwill		2,076
Equity		26,960
Profit for the year		370

Of all banks investigated here, Commerzbank has the highest risk in goodwill compared with the profit for the year. Goodwill reaches six times profit. However, it should be mentioned that the profit of Commerzbank was lower in 2014 than in 2015 because of restructuring processes following the acquisition of Dresdner Bank in 2009 and the financial crisis.

As an example of a big risk in goodwill, we will now have a look at Deutsche Bank.

Deutsche Bank: Discount rates 2014 (Annual report 2014, p. 440)

	Discount rate 2014	Discount rate 2013
Corporate Banking & Securities	14.5%	16.5%
Private & Business Clients	13.7%	14.3%
Global Transaction Banking	11.7%	13.1%
Deutsche Asset & Wealth Management	12.6%	12.8%
Non-Core Operating Units	14.8/14.5%	17.0/16.6%

Deutsche Bank uses high discount rates for all CGUs, compared to the other banks. The growth rate is the same for all CGUs, at 3.2% (Annual report 2014, p. 390).

If we compare the figures of Deutsche Bank with the banks above, Deutsche Bank seems to have less risk in these positions than the other banks.

	Discount rate minus growth rate 2014	Goodwill ($m)
Corporate Banking & Securities	11.3%	2,016
Private & Business Clients	10.5%	2,763
Global Transaction Banking	8.5%	474
Deutsche Asset & Wealth Management	9.4%	4,131
Total goodwill		9,518
Equity		73,223
Profit for the year		1,691

Until now, we only used equity, profit and goodwill itself for the analysis. Now we will include segment reporting data in the analysis (see chapter 4 for the problems with this).

Deutsche Bank reports for the two main segments Corporate Banking & Securities and Private & Business Clients a ROE (return on equity) of 13% and 9% (Annual report 2014, p. 24). Without checking this data we compare it with the cost of capital used for the impairment testing for the goodwill.

Deutsche Bank uses a cost of capital of 14.5% for Corporate Banking & Securities, but only reaches a ROE of 13%. For Private & Business Clients Deutsche Bank uses a cost of capital of 13.7%, but only reaches 9%. Both segments are not able to reach their cost of capital! This kind of disparity always indicates a problem in the goodwill if it is like this for a long period. Only looking at one year can lead to a misinterpretation, but the results of Deutsche Bank have not improved since the financial crisis! In third quarter 2015, Deutsche Bank finally impaired the goodwill of these two segments completely.

Another instructive example is the Royal Bank of Scotland in 2007. The following was said about impairment testing:

> "Further developments in the Group's US businesses have led to divisionalisation on a product basis instead of the geographical basis used in 2006. The recoverable amount was based on a value in use methodology using management forecasts to 2012 (2006 – 2014). A terminal growth rate of 5% (2006 – 5%) and a discount rate of 11% (2006 – 10%) was used. The recoverable amount of Citizens exceeds its carrying value by over \$5 billion. The profit growth rate would have to be approximately half the projected rate to cause the value in use of the unit to equal its carrying amount." (Royal Bank of Scotland, Annual Report 2007, S. 163).

The goodwill was 48,000 Mio. GBP in 2007, the discount rate minus growth rate was only 6% (11% – 5%). At that time, interest rates were much higher. This is only one example of the using of accounting rules to highlight problems in the financial statement of Royal Bank of Scotland in that year. As we know, Royal Bank of Scotland got into huge problems during the financial crisis.

Note

Goodwill can show us how risky the acquisition policy of a bank has been in the past. Because goodwill is not amortised over a special period anymore, banks only use impairments in bad times. Examples like Deutsche Bank or Royal Bank of Scotland show the big risk in this position and where you find a situation like this it has to be investigated very carefully.

3.2 Provisions

Provisions are made in the financial statement when past events lead to present legal or constructive obligations. These obligations have to be reliably estimated and an outflow of resources is expected.

The problem about provisions is that they can only be seen in the balance sheet if the bank expects the event to happen with a possibility of more than 50%.

Example

A customer takes a bank to court for a past event. The bank expects the possibility of losing to be 20%. The bank will make no provision in the balance sheet.

As long as a bank expects to win in court, it will show no provisions in the balance sheet. It has to show them only under contingent liabilities in the notes. Contingent liabilities have to be shown if the possibility of entry is more than remote but less than probable.

Normally, provisions are not a special position in the balance sheet which has to be investigated further. In previous years and still at the time of writing in 2016, they have a special meaning because of the several types of legal proceedings banks might have to deal with. Some of these types of proceedings are:

- Credit default swaps

- Interbank offered rates

- Mortgage-related securities matters

All banks mention other special contingent liabilities in their annual reports.

Example

In its 2014 annual report, Deutsche Bank mentions civil claims about former transactions of the acquired Bank Sal. Oppenheim (Annual report 2014, p. 401).

First, we analyse the provisions themselves. Here the cases are included where the bank already expects an outflow of resources.

Of special interest are the provisions for legal proceedings and regulatory matters. It is normal to have an amount in this position, even if the bank is not involved in bigger cases like the ones mentioned above.

Example

In its 2014 annual report, Erste Group mentions provisions for legal matters of 164 Mio. €, which come from normal bank business (Annual report 2014, p. 168).

These cases do not need to be investigated further if there are no big jumps in the amounts of provisions.

Example

In 2013, Erste Group has provisions for legal matters of 172 Mio. €, in 2014 it has provisions of 164 Mio. €. This is an absolutely normal case and there is no need to analyse it further (Annual report 2014, p. 168).

While banks normally have small amounts in provisions for legal matters, investment banks in particular have big problems at the moment because of fraud and other issues relating to their activities in recent years.

Example

In its 2014 annual report, Deutsche Bank reports an amount of 3,632 Mio. € for provisions for operational/litigation, compared to 2,106 Mio. € one year before in 2013 (Annual report 2014, p. 398).

Example

In its 2014 annual report, HSBC reports an amount of 1,832 Mio US-$ for provisions for legal proceedings and regulatory matters, compared to 2,184 Mio. US-$ one year before in 2013 (Annual report 2014, p. 421).

Note

The amount of provisions show us mostly if we have to further investigate contingent liabilities. It is always a good idea to have a look at this area, but in cases like Deutsche Bank or HSBC the notes should be read very carefully.

The influence of contingent liabilities can be shown by several examples from banks. Deutsche Bank published on 23/4/2015 an agreement to the joint settlement of all remaining investigations over interbank offered rate benchmarks with US and UK regulators.[2] This agreement cost 2,175 Mio. US-$ and 227 Mio. GBP with additional provisions of 1,500 Mio. € for 2015. This agreement was made just one month after the 2014 annual report was finished! With an amount of around 2,500 Mio. € to pay, Deutsche Bank had only provisions of 1,000 Mio. € for it. The provisions in the report were 60% (1,000 Mio. € = 40% of 2,500 Mio. €) less than the amount paid one month later. The provisions for operational/litigation at 31/12/2014 were 3,600 Mio. €. If all provisions were 60% too low, the real amount would be 9,000 Mio. €!

Is this only the worst case scenario? Do we have to include it in the analysis? For the third quarter 2015, Deutsche Bank announced an additional 1,000 Mio. € of litigation charges. The total amount of 3,600 Mio. € on 31/12/2014 had already grown to 7,600 Mio. € through the additional provision of 4,000 Mio. € in 2015. While provisions of 2,544 Mio. € were used in 2015, total provisions on 30/9/2015 reached around 5,200 Mio. € (7,600 Mio. € minus 2,544 Mio. € plus some smaller changes).[3]

In fact, the forecast based on 31/12/2014 (9,000 Mio. €), Deutsche Bank nearly reached in 2015. We will see in the future if this figure is

---

2. Deutsche Bank (bit.ly/2eQLAhD).
3. Deutsche Bank (bit.ly/2eLo6Mz).

now sufficient, or if Deutsche Bank has to provide more money for litigation charges.

This is only one example, but it shows the high risks banks could face in the positions of provisions and contingent liabilities!

Note

Provisions and contingent liabilities can include high risks, which are not yet included in the income statement. We always have to prove very carefully if there are any indications that banks made too little provision for their risks.

To put it another way, we can only get indications and not proof. We can only prove it several periods later.

Note

Was the financial crisis unpredictable? Maybe in the form it happened. But were the risks themselves unpredictable? No!

One of the first banks to fail was German IKB. In its annual report of 2006/7 it mentioned: "Other commitments include credit commitments totalling €11.9 billion (prior year: €11.2 billion) in favour of special purpose companies, which can only be utilised by these companies in case of a short-term liquidity squeeze." (Annual report 2006/07, p. 182.) IKB had total assets of €52 billion at that time. We are talking about guarantees of 20% of total assets! Were problems with short-term liquidity expected at that time? No, but 20% of total assets should make every analyst suspicious about what was happening here!

3.3 Deferred taxes

Deferred taxes arise mostly from differences between tax accounting and IFRS. Additionally, tax losses are part of deferred taxes, if they can be used by the bank in the near future. If use in the near future is not possible, they have to be mentioned in the notes.

Tax losses arise when a daughter company or the bank itself makes tax losses and can offset them with future profits. We cannot prove if the amount of tax losses in the balance sheet is right or wrong. But the additional information in the notes is a good source for investigating the profitability of the bank and its companies in the past.

Example

In its 2014 annual report, Erste Group reports that it has unused tax losses of 3,107 Mio. €. It does not expect to be able to use them in the near future so it cannot activate them (Annual report 2014, p. 161).

Example

In its 2014 annual report, HSBC reports unused tax losses in its US operations of 14,100 Mio. US-$ (Annual report 2014, p. 368).

Unused tax losses can also be used to influence the profit for the year. A change of future estimations about future profits changes the amount at which the unused taxes have to be activated.

Example

A bank has unused taxes of 2,000 Mio. €. For the near future it predicts a profit of 1,000 Mio. €. The tax rate is 40%. The bank has to activate 40% of 1,000 Mio. € (400 Mio. €), which increases the profit of the bank now. One year later (the profit of the year was 0), the estimation of near future profits increases to 1,500 Mio. €. Now 40% of 1,500 Mio. € (600 Mio. €) has to be activated. 200 Mio. € is the increase in the profit for the year!

One example of a huge effect of tax losses on profit comes from Commerzbank. The following table shows the profit with and without the effect of tax losses for 2010-2014.

Profit before and after taxes and corrected by influence of tax losses of Commerzbank 2010-2014

	2010	2011	2012	2013	2014
Profit before taxes	1,353	507	905	232	623
Income taxes	−136	−240	796	65	253
Profit after taxes	1,489	747	109	167	370
Change in unused taxes	−244	−500	−130	−163	−289
Profit after taxes before change in unused taxes	1,245	247	−21	4	81

We can see that the profit after taxes was determined in all years by the change in unused taxes. 2012 was only profitable because of the unused taxes, and 2013 was only very slightly profitable.

This is not proof that Commerzbank used unused taxes to increase its profit. But it suggests that we should have a very close look at the financial statement of Commerzbank to see if we can find any other indications that it used accounting policy to increase its profit.

Note

Unused taxes can be used to increase or lower profit. We should always check if there are any indications that the bank we are analysing used the accounting rules in such a way.

Note

Unused taxes are normal in bank business, but sometimes it is a good indicator for the success of a bank's expansion policy. Erste Group seems to have its tax losses in Eastern Europe, so it is an indicator that the expansion there has not been successful.

3.4 Level 3 Financial Instruments

Financial instruments are mostly valued according to IFRS at their fair value. There are three ways to calculate fair value:

1. If an active market exists, its price is used to calculate the fair value (Level 1).

2. If an active market does not exist, but the price can be calculated according to the price of an active market, the fair value is calculated by this (Level 2).

3. If 1 or 2 cannot be used, the fair value is calculated following the bank's own pricing models (Level 3).

Most financial instruments are calculated after level 1 or 2.

> ## Example
>
> HSBC values financial instruments after level 1 at 470 billion US-$, after level 2 at 591 billion US-$ and after level 3 at only 15 billion US-$ (Annual report 2014, p. 380).

It is often said that level 3 financial instruments contain a high risk. This is the result of the financial crisis when many financial instruments which were previously in level 1 or 2 moved to level 3 and dramatically lost value. We knew after 2008 that many financial instruments were valued too high. But it is not right to condemn level 3 financial instruments in general.

There are several analytical ways to treat level 3 financial instruments:

1. The worst case scenario: Level 3 papers are in general worthless so we subtract their total value from the equity and see if enough equity is left afterwards.

> ## Example
>
> HSBC has 15 billion US-$ of level 3 financial instruments (Annual report 2014, p. 380) and total equity of 200 billion US-$ (Annual

report 2014, p. 337). Even a full loss in value of all level 3 financial instruments would not be a problem for HSBC.

Example

Deutsche Bank has 31 billion € of level 3 financial instruments (Annual report 2014, p. 364) and total equity of 73 billion € (Annual report 2014, p. 315). A full loss would reduce equity significantly!

This analysis shows the impact of a level 3 financial instruments loss on the equity of the bank. Generally, the higher the percentage of level 3 compared to equity, the higher the risk of the bank.

2. The quality of level 3 financial instruments approach: In this approach we look for the earnings of the bank from the level 3 financial instruments in the past and try to figure out if these papers were profitable or not. If the papers were profitable, we can assume everything is also fine in the financial statement being analysed. If we find problems in the past, we have to be very careful about their value in the current financial statement.

Example

In 2014, HSBC had profits from level 3 financial instruments of 1,383 Mio. US-$ and in 2013 losses of 625 Mio. US-$ (Annual report 2014, pp. 384–385). For the period 2013-2014 there are no signs of problems in this position.

Example

In 2014, Deutsche Bank had profits from level 3 financial instruments of 2,233 Mio. € and in 2013 losses of 2,452 Mio. € (Annual report 2014, pp. 368–369). In comparison to HSBC, Deutsche Bank has a much higher value in level 3 financial instruments and for 2013–2014 there was a total loss from this.

As a result, HSBC has a much lower value in level 3 financial instruments and had a total profit in the period 2013–2014. There is some risk here, but compared to equity there is no sign of too much risk in this position. Deutsche Bank has a very high value in level 3 compared to equity and even a total loss from 2013–2014. This is a warning sign in the analysis, although it is not possible to say if the risk is high or not.

4. Analysis of Segment Reporting

4.1 Meaningfulness of segment reporting for banks

Segment reporting is widely used in the analysis of banks and non-banks. Its task is to show the reader of financial statements which segments of a company are profitable and which not, or which are more profitable than others, how much business the segments do with each other, and so on. Segment reporting is a very important aspect of analysis of non-banks.

For banks, segment reporting has several problems. Accounting policy can easily be used for it, so by using accounting rules in particular ways, completely different results can be shown. The results shown in the segment reporting have to be viewed with caution because of this.

First, a big part of interest earnings comes from maturity transformation. Normally banks do not refinance all assets with the same maturity. The normal maturity structure of a bank shows for liabilities much more short-term liabilities than short-term loans on the asset side. In a normal yield (normal yield means higher duration = higher interest rate), the higher the disparity in maturity, the higher the interest income.

Example

Barclays (Annual report 2014, p. 205) reports the following maturities of assets and liabilities:

	Assets	Liabilities
On demand	630,152	811,066
Not more than three months	254,892	275,500
Over three but less six months	25,909	30,194
Over six but less nine months	13,519	22,588
Over nine months less one year	12,579	13,572
Over one year less two years	49,789	20,011
Over two years less three years	43,303	18,117
Over three years less five years	60,418	23,236
Over five years less ten years	79,386	29,953
Over ten years	151,583	18,233

Up to one year, liabilities always exceed assets; over one year assets always exceed liabilities. Barclays – like most banks – refinances long-term assets partly with short-term liabilities.

As normal as maturity transformation is in bank business, a big problem comes from the fair distribution of the earnings from the maturity transformation for the different segments. Most banks do not report their method for distributing these earnings across the different segments.

For example, the VP Bank Group from Lichtenstein reports that earnings from maturity transformation are in the segment 'Corporate Center'.[4] The operating segments of this bank do not include earnings from maturity transformation. For the banks analysed in this book,

---

4. VP Bank (bit.ly/2ear1wH).

we mostly do not find information about earnings from maturity transformation. So the earnings from maturity transformation may be distributed over the operating segments too.

The problem is that there is no fair way to distribute these earnings over segments and banks may distribute earnings in such a way that they make some segments look better than they really are. We do not know, so segment reporting cannot be used for analysis in the same way as the income statement or the balance sheet.

The problem of earnings from maturity transformation is significant enough to not trust the data shown in segment reporting, but there are several other problems as well.

A second problem is that comparisons between different banks is mostly not possible, because banks build segments in different ways.

Third, inter-segment business is calculated differently. Lloyds, for example, recharges inter-segment services generally at cost with some exceptions (Annual report 2014, p. 77). Commerzbank uses risk-free interest for inter-segment business (Annual report 2014, p. 195).

Example

Commerzbank reports the following values for equity distributed to its segments (Annual report 2014, p. 197):

Private Customers	3,956
Mittelstandsbank	6,926
Central & Eastern Europe	1,587
Corporates & Markets	4,193
Non-Core Assets	7,606

The highest equity is distributed to the Non-Core Assets. Because the interest on equity is calculated by a risk-free interest rate, Non-Core Assets gets a smaller interest income than by choosing a risk-adequate interest rate. By using this method, Commerzbank reports a less good operating profit or loss for this segment than by using a risk-adequate interest rate. As a result, Non-Core Assets report a ROE of −11.1%. Using a risk-adequate interest rate, the ROE would have been much better. If the risk-adequate interest rate was 11%, the segment would report a profit/loss of around 0%.

Example

HSBC reports the following assets and liabilities for its segments (Annual report 2014, p. 375):

	Assets	Liabilities
Europe	1,290,926	1,223,371
Asia	878,723	807,998
MENA	62,417	52,569
North America	436,859	398,356
Latin America	115,354	102,007

All segments have higher assets than liabilities. The difference is the equity of HSBC, which is separated over the several segments of the bank.

Commerzbank reports the following assets and liabilities for its segments (Annual report 2014, p. 197):

	Assets	Liabilities
Private Customers	72,577	101,963
Mittelstandsbank	89,691	136,138
Central & Eastern Europe	27,657	22,945
Corporates & Markets	184,734	163,637
Non-Core Assets	102,849	67,889

Three segments have higher assets than liabilitites, two lower. The first two segments get financed by the other three. If a low interest rate is used, the first two segments get a higher profit, if a high interest rate is used, the other three have a higher profit. It is not reported how the interest rate is calculated.

The highest operating profit was made by Mittelstandsbank, the segment with the biggest difference between liabilities and assets. Every 1% less interest rate for their liabilities costs 470 Mio. € of profit. The reported profit is 1,217 Mio. €.

Especially in modern times, in which segment profits are used in newspapers and other sources, it is very important for banks to show the profits analysts expect. Whether these profits are 'real' or made by segment accounting policy cannot be answered from the external view of the analyst. But it should make the analyst very careful about interpreting too much from the segment reporting data.

Example

Commerzbank reports the following operating profits/losses for its segments (Annual report 2014, p. 197):

	Operating Profit/Loss
Private Customers	420
Mittelstandsbank	1,217
Central & Eastern Europe	364
Corporates & Markets	675
Non-Core Assets	-786
Others and Consolidation	-1,206

The four operating segments all have more or less high profits, while the non-core assets and the consolidation have high losses. The whole bank reports a profit of 684 Mio. €.

> HSBC has a consolidation segment too. Its profit/loss in 2014 was 0 (Annual report 2014, p. 372).

Some banks follow the HSBC method (for example Santander), some use the Commerzbank method (for example UniCredit). This data is not comparable.

Segment reporting is mainly interesting in that it reveals what a bank wants to show. It should never be overinterpreted, because banks have too much influence on the way the information is presented.

4.2 Segment reporting ratios

As mentioned in the previous chapter, segment reporting is widely used in the accounting policies of banks. Segment data is often used in newspapers and other sources to describe bank results. This means it is useful to be aware of the core ratios of segment reporting and that is what we will look at here.

The importance of a segment for the bank can be measured in different ways:

percentage of bank profit = segment profit for the year / bank profit for the year

percentage of bank operating income = segment operating income for the year / bank operating income for the year

Example

HSBC reports the following segment profits/losses and operating income (Annual report 2014, p. 372):

	Profit/Loss	Operating income
Europe	−257	21,571
Asia	12,083	23,677
MENA	1,487	2,548
North America	1,222	8,152
Latin America	170	8,272
Total	14,705	61,248

	Percentage of bank profit	Percentage of bank operating income
Europe	−2%	35%
Asia	82%	39%
MENA	10%	4%
North America	8%	13%
Latin America	1%	14%

Note on the table: The total row is not the sum of segments because some amounts (for example, corporate center) are not included in the table.

Asia is the most important segment with 82% of the bank's profit. Europe has high operating income, but because of very high operating expenses there is a loss at the end.

MENA (Middle East and North Africa), North America and Latin America have only small importance following the segment reporting.

These two ratios show the importance of each segment for bank profits and income. Another ratio which can be calculated is:

percentage of bank assets = segment assets / bank assets

And similarly for liabilities:

percentage of bank liabilities = segment liabilities / bank liabilities

Example

HSBC reports the following segment assets/liabilities (Annual report 2014, p. 372):

	Assets	Liabilities
Europe	1,290,926	1,223,371
Asia	878,723	807,998
MENA	62,417	52,569
North America	436,859	398,356
Latin America	115,354	102,007
Total	2,634,139	2,434,161

	Percentage of bank assets	Percentage of bank liabilities
Europe	49%	50%
Asia	33%	33%
MENA	2%	2%
North America	17%	16%
Latin America	4%	4%

Note on the table: Total is not sum of segments because intersegment assets and liabilities had to be subtracted to get the total amount.

HSBC does most business in the Europe segment, followed by Asia and North America. MENA and Latin America have only low importance.

Combined with the profit and operating income ratios, the Asia segment makes higher operating income with less assets and liabilities than the Europe segment. Also North America is a big segment by assets and liabilities, but poor in profits.

MENA is poor in assets and liabilities, but strong in profits.

What implications can we draw from these ratios?

The ratios show – notwithstanding all the problems described in chapter 4.1 – which segments are most important for a bank and which segments have least importance; and in which segments a bank should invest and where it should use less capital.

Example

The losses HSBC makes in Europe combined with the very high capital used there (difference assets – liabilities = equity = 67.5 billion US-$), gives the implication that HSBC should reduce business in Europe and strengthen it in Asia.

Sometimes, these implications can fail. The synergistic effects between two segments cannot always be seen from the segment reporting. We get the implication that capital should be transferred from segment A to segment B, but maybe the customers in both segments are mostly similar and cutting back business in segment A means automatically losing business in segment B.

The problems of the efficiency ratio (cost-income ratio) are discussed in chapter 5.2. Because we have no better ratio, it is used in segment analysis:

segment efficiency ratio = segment operating expenses / segment net operating income before loan impairment

Example

HSBC reports the following segment operating expenses/net operating income (Annual report 2014, p. 372):

	Operating Expenses	Net Operating Income
Europe	20,217	21,571
Asia	10,427	23,677
MENA	1,216	2,548
North America	6,429	8,152
Latin America	5,932	8,272

The segment efficiency ratios are:

Europe	93.7%
Asia	44.0%
MENA	47.7%
North America	78.9%
Latin America	71.7%

As with the ratios before, again Asia and MENA have the best ratios, while Europe and North America are far behind.

Another ratio for segment reporting looks at the income sources of a segment. The three main income sources are:

1. Net interest income
2. Net fee income
3. Net trading income

Additionally, 'other income' is also included in net operating income.

For every income source we can calculate a ratio:

percentage of net interest income = net interest income / net operating income

percentage of net fee income = net fee income / net operating income

percentage of net trading income = net trading income / net operating income

percentage of other income = other income / net operating income

Example

UniCredit reports the following information in its segment reporting (Annual report 2014, p. 497):

	Net interest	Net fees	Net trading	Other income
Commercial Banking Italy	5,037	3,318	−4	−23
Commercial Banking Germany	1,275	831	−20	90
Commercial Banking Austria	723	516	186	31
Poland	1,066	494	162	21
Central Eastern Europe	2,495	760	255	54
Corporate & Investment Banking	2,301	506	881	-59
Asset Management	2	769	1	14
Asset Gathering	228	195	30	−3

The ratios are as follows:

	Net interest (%)	Net fees (%)	Net trading (%)	Other income (%)
Commercial Banking Italy	60%	40%	0%	0%
Commercial Banking Germany	66%	32%	−1%	3%
Commercial Banking Austria	50%	35%	13%	2%
Poland	61%	28%	9%	1%
Central Eastern Europe	70%	21%	7%	2%
Corporate & Investment Banking	63%	14%	24%	−2%
Asset Management	0%	98%	0%	2%
Asset Gathering	51%	43%	7%	−1%

Because UniCredit has separated the segments partly in a functional way, Asset Management has mostly fees and Corporate & Investment Banking has a high percentage of net trading. The first five segments are regional, so in each of these there is a high percentage of net interest and net fees.

It depends mainly on the structure of a segment, how high its ratios are. In a regional segment structure (like HSBC), all segments will have net interest income, net fee income and net trading income. In a functional structure, net fee income and net trading income will be concentrated in one or only a few segments.

5. Ratios for Bank Financial Statement Analysis

There are several ratios which can be used for bank financial statement analysis. I will discuss here those ratios which are most widely used.

5.1 Return-on ratios

The main ratio for financial statement analysis is Return on Equity (RoE), which is calculated in the following way:

return on equity (RoE) = net income / net shareholder equity

RoE is widely used among banks as a strategic goal (for example, Barclays aims to achieve an adjusted RoE above 12% by 2016, Banco Santander publishes its RoE in its financial statements, and so on).

In fact, RoE is not a good measurement for the performance of a bank. While equity can be used in non-banks for their whole business, banks cannot do this because of special banking regulations. The equity of a bank is used, for example, for the goodwill too. Goodwill has to be deducted from the equity to calculate the tier 1 capital, so this amount is not available for underlying risk-weighted assets. If we calculate RoE, we do not measure the performance of the bank, but the return for the shareholders, independent of what the shareholders' equity is used for – if it is used for goodwill, for example, it is not used in bank business.

A much better ratio than the RoE to measure bank performance is the ROTE – Return on Tangible Equity. It measures the return on the tangible common equity. Tangible common shareholders' equity equals the total shareholders' equity less preferred stock, goodwill, and identifiable intangible assets. With this ratio, the main critiques of RoE for banks are solved. But even the ROTE does not give the return on the capital which can be used for bank business.

Tier 1 capital is the capital amount for bank business, which limits the risks a bank can take. To measure the performance of a bank, the tier 1 capital is the decisive capital amount. We can define the Return on Tier 1 capital (ROTC) as follows:

ROTC = operating income / tier 1 capital

Tier 1 capital is equal to the tier 1 capital ratio multiplied by risk-weighted-assets:

ROTC = operating income / (tier 1 capital ratio × risk-weighted assets)

ROTC = (operating income / risk-weighted assets) × (1 / tier 1 capital ratio)

The return on risk-weighted assets (RoRWA) is:

RoRWA = operating income / risk-weighted assets

ROTC = RoRWA × (1 / tier 1 capital ratio)

The return on tier 1 capital can be separated into two parts: the return on risk-weighted assets (RoRWA) and the reciprocal of the tier 1 capital ratio.

> ### Note
>
> While most banks use the term risk-weighted assets, some banks replace it with the risk exposure amount. In this book, the term risk-weighted assets is used.

The ROTC can be easily strengthened or weakened by changing the tier 1 capital ratio, for example by buying shares back or selling new shares. The ROTC is in fact only partly to do with the real performance of a bank, but is also related to the capital structure. The ROTC is similar to the ROE for non-banks. And so the RoRWA is similar to the ROA (return-on-assets). The RoRWA is the ratio showing the real performance of the bank's business, independent from the capital structure.

> ### Example
>
> The example bank has in Year Z a ROTC of 10% with a RoRWA of 2% and a tier 1 capital ratio of 20%. In the following year, the tier 1 capital ratio drops to 10% as a result of the bank buying its own shares, while the RoRWA drops to 1.5%. The ROTC in this year is 15% (1.5% × 110%). Only comparing the ROTC, we could get the impression that the bank is stronger now. In fact, the RoRWA has dropped significantly, so the performance of the bank's business is weaker than the year before.

Whether or not it is appropriate to calculate risk-weighted assets can be widely discussed. In fact, it limits the business a bank can make. For banking supervision, banks can use equity only once for risk-weighted assets. Whether or not it is right or wrong to calculate the risk-weighted assets is not relevant to the analysis of the bank, because this is what is used by banking supervision.

The RoRWA has several advantages:

- It makes banks with different strategies comparable.

Example

Typical ratios like interest margin do not work well for comparing different kinds of banks, such as investment banks, mortgage banks or public finance banks. With the RoRWA different types of banks are directly comparable. For example, mortgage loans have a lower interest margin than customer loans, but by including the risk-weight factors we can see if mortgage financing is more profitable than customer loans, and so on.

- The risk-weighted assets directly represent the limiting factor of bank business – equity. With the RoRWA we follow a controlled approach for how to manage the equity!
- The RoRWA can be calculated for every single part of business that a bank is doing, so it is not only a ratio for the external analysis, but for the internal accounting too.

Example

The example bank has an equity of 100 and can decide between the following loans:

	Risk-weight	Nominal value	Interest margin
Mortgage loan	40%	3,000	1%
Customer loan	90%	1,000	2%

The tier 1 capital ratio is 8%. So the mortgage loan has an equity demand of $3,000 \times 40\% \times 8\% = 96$ and the customer loan an equity demand of $1,000 \times 90\% \times 8\% = 72$. The RoRWAs for the two loans are:

Mortgage loan $= 2.5\%$

Customer loan $= 2.22\%$

The mortgage loan is the better alternative.

There are some disadvantages with RoRWA too, which come from the problems of risk-weighted assets in general:

- The risk-weighted assets may not always show the risk of an asset, for example the Greek public debt was included in risk-weighted assets with a very small percentage. Banks tend to do regulatory capital arbitrage to invest their money in businesses that have low amounts in risk-weighted assets.

Example

The example bank can invest its money in two different kinds of loans:

	Rating	Risk-weight
Public debt	BBB	20%
Customer loan	AAA	100%

For the same amount of equity, the bank can invest five times more capital in the public debt than in the customer loan, while the risk of the customer loan is much lower than for the public debt. The effect is that banks tend to invest in public debt because the estimated return on the invested equity is much higher.

- Correlation effects are not included in the risk-weighted assets in the standard approach so the regulatory capital arbitrage can lead to effects not wanted by banking supervision.

Example

In the last example, the concentration risk of the public debt loan is much higher than for the customer loan which uses the same amount of equity.

RoRWA for the Stoxx 600 Banks

Before making further analysis, the table below shows the RoRWA for all banks of the Stoxx 600 Banks. This enables you to get a feeling for the different values this ratio has with real banks.

Name	Profit before tax from continuing operations	Risk-weighted assets	RoRWA
Banca Carige	−793	20,474	−3.87%
Banca Monte dei Paschi	−2,060	76,220	−2.70%
Banco Bilbao Vizcaya Argentaria (BBVA)	3,980	637,572	0.62%
Banco Comercial Portugues	−955	42,376	−2.25%
Banco de Sabadell	486	74,418	0.65%
Banco Popolare	−2,800	47,987	−5.83%
Banco Popular	373	80,113	0.47%
Banco Santander	9,720	585,243	1.66%
Bank of Ireland	920	51,600	1.78%
Bankia	912	88,565	1.03%
Bankinter	393	25,704	1.53%
Barclays	2,702	440,000	0.61%
Banca Popolare di Sondrio	25	21,338	0.12%
Banca Popolare dell'Emilia Romagna	58	40,692	0.14%
BNP Paribas	3,149	619,827	0.51%
Caixabank	202	139,729	0.14%
Commerzbank	623	215,200	0.29%
Credit Suisse	3,627	291,490	1.24%
Crédit Agricole	7,763	494,934	1.57%
Danske Bank	7,835	866,000	0.90%

Name	Profit before tax from continuing operations	Risk-weighted assets	RoRWA
Deutsche Bank	3,116	396,648	0.79%
DNB	27,102	1,121,000	2.42%
Erste Group Bank	378	100,600	0.38%
HSBC	18,680	1,219,765	1.53%
Intesa Sanpaolo	3,009	269,790	1.12%
Julius Bär	470	16,978	2.77%
Jyske Bank	3,103	176,433	1.76%
KBC	1,708	91,236	1.87%
Komercni Banka	16,030	384,186	4.17%
Lloyds	1,762	240,000	0.73%
Mediobanca	757	59,577	1.27%
National Bank of Greece	−1,422	60,303	−2.36%
Natixis	1,838	115,200	1.60%
Nordea Bank	4,324	220,413	1.96%
Raiffeisen	23	68,721	0.03%
Royal Bank of Scotland	2,643	355,900	0.74%
SEB	13,376	616,531	2.17%
Société Générale	4,375	353,196	1.24%
Standard Chartered	4,235	341,648	1.24%
Svenska Handelsbanken	17,524	480,388	3.65%
Swedbank	21,026	414,000	5.08%
Sydbank	1,329	72,500	1.83%
UBS	2,461	216,462	1.14%
UniCredit	4,091	409,223	1.00%
UBI Unione di Banche	−776	61,763	−1.26%

The average RoRWA is 0.90%. Some Italian banks have a negative RoRWA, while Swedbank with more than 5% has the highest, followed by Komercni Banka. Both Swedbank and Komercni Banka are small, compared to the big players like HSBC or Banco Santander. The same is true for Svenska Handelsbanken (no. 3) and Julius Bär (no. 4).

It seems as if small banks can reach a higher RoRWA than big banks. The reasons for this can only be estimated: maybe the regional markets the banks operate in (mainly Sweden, and the Czech Republic for Julius Bär) are very focused on asset management.

Thinking about market capitalisation, the biggest banks (HSBC, Lloyds, Banco Santander, UBS, Barclays) have a RoRWA between 0.61% and 1.66%, mostly around the average of 0.90%. Barclays and Lloyds lie beneath the average, HSBC and Banco Santander far above it.

As for the Swedish and Czech banks, again here it may be that the regional markets are the reason. But the other Spanish and UK banks have much lower RoRWAs, so – without further analysis – it seems to be the strategy HSBC and Banco Santander are following that is responsible for their RoRWA figures.

Interest, trade and operating ratios

The risk-weighted assets are the sum of:

- Credit risk
- Operational risk
- Market risk

It is a rule for every ratio that the numerator and denominator must have a meaningful relationship. The following ratios do not fully reach this relationship, but we can assume that:

- Credit risk leads to interest income
- Market risk leads to trade income
- Operational risk leads to operating expenses

In this way we can calculate:

- interest ratio = net interest income / credit risk
- trade ratio = net trading income / market risk
- operating ratio = operating expenses / operational risk

For the interest ratio and trade ratio higher is better, for the operating ratio lower is better.

Example

Standard Chartered has the following values:

Net interest income	11,003
Net trading income	1,896
Operating expenses	11,046
Credit risk	296,246
Market risk	20,295
Operational risk	35,107

interest ratio = 11,003 / 292,246 = 3.76%

trade ratio = 1,896 / 20,295 = 9.34%

operating ratio = 11,046 / 35,107 = 31.46%

We compare these ratios with Deutsche Bank:

Net interest income	14,272
Net trading income	4,407
Operating expenses	27,699
Credit risk	262,678
Market risk	64,209
Operational risk	67,082

interest ratio = 14,272 / 262,678 = 5.43%

trade ratio = 4,407 / 64,209 = 6.86%

operating ratio = 27,699 / 67,082 = 41.29%

While the interest ratio of Deutsche Bank is better than that of Standard Chartered, Standard Chartered has better values for the trade ratio and operating ratio. This is remarkable because Deutsche Bank is an investment bank so we would expect a higher trade ratio, while Standard Chartered is mainly a credit bank so we would expect a higher interest ratio.

The higher operating ratio of Deutsche Bank seems to be attributable to high legal risks in 2014, which led to high costs.

Return-on-assets

Finally, we can calculate a return-on-assets (ROA) ratio:

return-on-assets = (net income + tax expenses + interest expenses) / total assets

Example

HSBC reports the following data (Annual report 2014, pp. 335, 337):

Profit for the year	14,705
Tax expense	3,975
Interest expense	16,250
Total assets	2,634,139

return-on-assets = (14,705 + 3,975 + 16,250) / 2,634,139 = 1.33%

Normally, the ROA is not mentioned as a good ratio for a bank. In fact, it has some advantages. More so than for non-banks, the leverage effect has a strong meaning for banks. Banks have a much lower equity ratio than non-banks, so it is extremely important to have a ROA that is higher than the cost of liabilities.

First of all, we define the leverage effect:

ROE = ROA + (liabilities / assets) × (ROA − cost of liabilities)

As long as the ROA is higher than the cost of liabilities, the bank will benefit from high leverage. But if the difference between ROA and cost of liabilities turns negative, the ROE will fall rapidly. Because a bank's equity ratio is not high compared to non-banks, it can very quickly lead to bankruptcy when ROE turns negative.

The ROA can be compared with the ROA of other banks, but especially with the bank's own cost of liabilities:

cost of liabilities = interest expense / total liabilities

Example

HSBC reports the following data (Annual report 2014, pp. 335, 337):

Interest expense	16,250
Total liabilities	2,434,161

cost of liabilities = 16,250 / 2,434,161 = 0.67%

While the cost of liabilities of HSBC is 0.67%, the ROA reaches 1.33%. HSBC has a positive effect from the leverage on its ROE.

5.2 Efficiency ratio (Cost-income ratio)

A commonly used ratio when analysing a bank is the efficiency ratio. It is calculated as follows:

efficiency ratio = operating expenses / net operating income before loan impairment charges

The lower the efficiency ratio, the better.

Example

HSBC reports its cost efficiency ratio at 67.3% in 2014 (Annual report 2014, p. 3).

Most banks state in their annual reports that their goal is to achieve an efficiency ratio from 50%–60% (for example, HSBC mid-50% (Annual report 2014, p. 32), Royal Bank of Scotland <50% (Annual report 2014, p. 13)).

As common as the efficiency ratio – or cost-income ratio – is, it faces many problems in achieving the task analysts ask of it.

As mentioned before, in every ratio the numerator and denominator must have a meaningful relationship. We have to question if the whole net operating income of a bank depends on the operating expenses. In fact, some parts of the net operating income do not depend on the operating expenses:

- The higher the equity of a bank, the better the efficiency ratio will be. Equity does not lead to interest expenses so the more equity a bank uses, the higher the net operating income will be. Because the operating expenses will stay the same, the efficiency ratio will get lower, which is better! This has nothing to do with a better efficiency, but may be the result of an uneconomic use of equity.

Example

Svenska Handelsbanken has in 2014 a tier 1 capital ratio of 20.4% and an efficiency ratio of 45.2% (Annual report 2014, p. 1). Both ratios improved compared to 2013. The tier 1 capital ratio was 18.9% in 2013, and the efficiency ratio 47.0% (Annual report 2014, p. 1). Is the decrease in efficiency ratio a reliable indicator of a better efficiency, or is it only a reliable indicator of a greater use of equity compared to the year before?

Example

Svenska Handelsbanken has in 2014 a tier 1 capital ratio of 20.4% and an efficiency ratio of 45.2% (Annual report 2014, p. 1). Raiffeisen has in 2014 a tier 1 capital ratio of 10.9% and an efficiency ratio of 56.5% (Annual report 2014, p. 3). Does Svenska Handelsbanken really have a higher efficiency than Raiffeisen, or does the lower efficiency ratio only point to a higher tier 1 capital ratio?

- The efficiency ratio is calculated with net operating income before loan impairment charges. This leads to the abstruse situation that the more credit risks a bank takes, the lower the efficiency ratio will be (if credit risks are fairly priced).

Example

UniCredit has in 2014 an efficiency ratio of 61.5% (Annual report 2014, p. 20), while there were losses on impairment of loans of 4,178 Mio. € with loans to customers of 470,569 Mio. €, so impairment of 0.89% of all customer loans in 2014 (Annual report 2014, pp. 88, 90). Commerzbank has in 2014 an efficiency ratio of 79.1% (Annual report 2014, p. U2), while there were losses on impairment of loans of 1,144 Mio. € with loans to customers of 232,867 Mio. €, so impairment of 0.49% of all customer loans in 2014 (Annual report 2014, pp. 147, 150). Does the better efficiency ratio of UniCredit really show better efficiency, or does it only show higher interest income through taking higher credit risk combined with higher impairment on loans?

- Normally banks do not refinance all assets with the same maturity. The normal maturity structure shows for liabilities much more short-term liabilities than short-term loans on the asset side. In a normal yield, the higher the disparity in maturity, the higher the interest income and so the lower the efficiency ratio. These so-called earnings from maturity transformation have nothing to do with the efficiency of a bank, so in fact they should be eliminated from the efficiency ratio. But because banks do not publish their earnings from maturity transformation, we cannot do that in external analysis.

As shown, the efficiency ratio has many disadvantages which mean it is not a good ratio for measuring the efficiency of a bank. Unfortunately, we cannot calculate a better ratio from the data of financial statements. That is the reason the efficiency ratio is widely used; not because it is a good ratio to measure efficiency.

When interpreting the efficiency ratio, its disadvantages always have to be considered.

5.3 Ratios for loan loss provisions

5.3.1 Allocation ratio

The allocation ratio is the ratio of the net loan loss provisions to the average total lending:

allocation ratio = net loan loss provisions / average total lending

total lending = loans to banks + loans to customers

Average total lending is calculated as the average of the end-value of this year and the end-value of last year.

The ratio shows which part of the total lending has to be impaired in the period.

Example

Standard Chartered reports in 2014 loan impairment charges and other credit risk provisions of 2,141 Mio. US-$ (Annual report 2014, p. 225). Loans and advances to banks are 83,890 Mio. US-$ (31.12.2013: 83,702 Mio. US-$), loans and advances to customers are 284,695 Mio. US-$ (31.12.2013: 290,708 Mio. US-$) (Annual report 2014, p. 227).

Average total lending is: (83,890 + 83,702 + 284,695 + 290,708) / 2 = 371,498

The allocation ratio is:

allocation ratio = 2,141 / 371,498 = 0.58%

Example

Commerzbank reports in 2014 loan impairment charges and other credit risk provisions of 1,144 Mio. € (Annual report 2014, p. 147). Loans and advances to banks are 80,036 Mio. € (31.12.2013: 87,545 Mio. €), loans and advances to customers are 232,867 Mio. € (31.12.2013: 245,938 Mio. €) (Annual report 2014, p. 337).

Average total lending is: (80,036 + 87,545 + 232,867 + 245,938) / 2 = 323,193

The allocation ratio is:

allocation ratio = 1,144 / 323,193 = 0.35%

How should the allocation ratio be interpreted?

Comparing Commerzbank and Standard Chartered, Commerzbank looks much better. By only looking at the allocation ratio we could get the impression that Commerzbank is the less risky bank and may be more profitable than Standard Chartered.

First of all, *the allocation ratio* always has to be compared with the net interest margin. A high allocation rate is not automatically bad if the bank is able to get a much higher interest margin. We will have a further look at the interest margin later, but for now we just calculate it from the income statement:

net interest margin = net interest income / average total lending

Example

Standard Chartered reports in 2014 net interest income of 11,003 Mio. US-$ (Annual report 2014, p. 225). Average total lending is 371,498 Mio. US-$.

net interest margin = 11,003 / 371,498 = 2.96%

Commerzbank reports in 2014 net interest income of 5,607 Mio. € (Annual report 2014, p. 147). Average total lending is 323,193 Mio. €.

net interest margin = 5,607 / 323,193 = 1.73%

As we can see, Standard Chartered has a little higher allocation rate than Commerzbank, but the net interest margin is much higher. The allocation rate alone has nearly no meaning – it always has to be analysed including the net interest margin!

The second problem of the allocation rate is its fluctuation over time. The allocation rate changes from year to year, depending on the economic situation, bank policy or just luck. The one-year-allocation rate can be very good, but when analysed over a longer time period it can be much worse. If the allocation rate is used in the analysis, it should always be used as a long-term average.

The long-term average has the advantage that short-time influences like a very good or a very bad economic situation do not have a big influence on the data.

The last problem is that banks tend to impair too much in bad economic times so they have to release this in later periods. A comparison between releases and impairments can show how careful banks are or how much they use impairments for accounting policy.

5.3.2 Default ratio

The default ratio is the relationship of credit defaults with average total lending:

default ratio = credit defaults / average total lending

total lending = loans to banks + loans to customers

Average total lending is calculated as the average of the end-value of this year and the end-value of last year.

The default ratio shows which part of the total lending has really defaulted in the period. Impairment is made when a bank assumes that a customer cannot pay back its loan. Default is when the loan really does not get paid back at the moment the contract ends. Impairment can be made by accounting policy, default cannot.

Example

Commerzbank reports in 2014 utilisation of loan loss provisions of 1,956 Mio. € (Annual report 2014, p. 203). Loans and advances to banks are 80,036 Mio. € (31.12.2013: 87,545 Mio. €), loans and advances to customers are 232,867 Mio. € (31.12.2013: 245,938 Mio. €) (Annual report 2014, p. 337).

Average total lending is: (80,036 + 87,545 + 232,867 + 245,938) / 2 = 323,193

The default ratio is:

default ratio = 1,956 / 323,193 = 0.61%

For some banks, credit defaults have to be calculated indirectly because they do not publish this information. The loan loss provision for a year is calculated by:

loan loss provisions from the year before + net loan loss provision – utilisation = loan loss provisions of this year

All data except utilisation is known, so:

utilisation = loan loss provisions from the year before + net loan loss provision – loan loss provisions of this year

Example

Standard Chartered reports the following data:

Loan loss provisions from the year before	3,547 (Annual report 2013, pp. 276, 277)
Net loan loss provision	2,141 (Annual report 2014, p. 225)
Loan loss provisions of this year	4,073 (Annual report 2014, p. 275)

utilisation = loan loss provisions from the year before + net loan loss provision - loan loss provisions of this year

utilisation = 3,547 + 2,141 – 4,073 = 1,615

With this data we can calculate the default risk too.

Example

As calculated, Standard Chartered has had utilisation of 1,615 Mio. US-$ in 2014. Loans and advances to banks are

83,890 Mio. US-$ (31.12.2013: 83,702 Mio. US-$), loans and advances to customers are 284,695 Mio. US-$ (31.12.2013: 290,708 Mio. US-$) (Annual report 2014, p. 227).

Average total lending is: (83,890 + 83,702 + 282,695 + 290,708) / 2 = 371,498

The default ratio is:

default ratio = 1,615 / 370,498 = 0.44%

How should the default rate be interpreted?

Again, it always has to be compared with the net interest margin. A high default rate is not automatically bad if the bank is able to get a much higher interest margin. Like the allocation rate, the default rate fluctuates over time. It changes from year to year, depending on the economic situation, bank policy or just luck. If the default rate is used in the analysis, it should always be used as a long-term average.

The following table shows the default rate for the example of Commerzbank from 1997 to 2014.

Table: Default rate of Commerzbank 1997 to 2014

	Defaults in (€m)	Total lending (€m)	Default rate
1997	808	185,323	0.44%
1998	447	207,555	0.22%
1999	329	223,243	0.15%
2000	841	239,731	0.35%
2001	679	278,059	0.24%
2002	817	197,481	0.41%
2003	818	184,585	0.44%
2004	1,005	209,679	0.48%
2005	794	234,696	0.34%

	Defaults in (€m)	Total lending (€m)	Default rate
2006	1,015	316,472	0.32%
2007	1,781	316,562	0.56%
2008	1,507	313,653	0.48%
2009	1,965	368,401	0.53%
2010	2,438	330,316	0.74%
2011	1,947	303,913	0.64%
2012	1,259	272,848	0.46%
2013	1,450	246,716	0.59%
2014	1,956	323,193	0.61%
Average			0.45%

We can see that the fluctuation of the default rate over this period is very high. It is lowest in 1999 (0.15%) and highest in 2010 (0.74%). On average, Commerzbank has a default rate of 0.45%. If there are no special influences on the default rates in particular years, 0.45% is the best prediction for the average default rate in the near future.

At this point, we can pause to discuss the goal of the analysis. Mostly, analysts tend to see the near future as being as good or as bad as the current year. Because of this, share price forecasts for banks tend to be over- or underestimated compared to the fair price. In boom periods, the very low defaults and net loan loss provisions are forecast for the future and high share prices are predicted. In recession, the very high defaults and net loan loss provisions are forecast for the future and very low share prices are predicted.

In this book, we will predict an average, estimated operating income for a bank. As mentioned in the introduction, this is much more possible for a bank than for a non-bank, because most earnings and expenses for the next period are already safe. For this, we need the average estimated operating income and not a very high or a very low one.

It is the case that high net loan loss provisions can lead to bankruptcy. But, a strong bank is much more likely able to survive that situation than a bank which also suffers in normal times.

The banks which failed in the world financial crisis were all weak banks in normal times. From this point of view, an analysis based on normal times can show the kind of bank that will get into problems first in a recession or even a financial crisis. This was covered above, but it is so important to repeat here that this does not mean that this kind of bank will fail first. Bank failures depend on other circumstances too. Maybe specific banks have a special significance for local politics and local businesses and have to be saved. This is not the kind of question we can answer with analysis of financial statements.

The default rate has advantages compared to the allocation rate. First of all, the allocation rate is more easily influenced by accounting policy. A default is a default, while the reasons for a net loan loss provision are not as clear as for a default.

Second, the default rate is normally the basis for banks' pricing of credit risk. Using the default rate, we are able to 'copy' the internal calculation. Last, the default rate does not vary as much as the allocation rate. It is much more stable, so it is better for use in external analysis.

In the long run, using the average allocation rate or average default rate makes no difference. Loan loss provisions either lead to a default, or – if the reason for the loan loss provision does not exist anymore – they will be resolved.

5.3.3 Provision cover ratio

The provision cover ratio is the relationship between total loan loss provisions and total lending:

provision cover ratio = total loan loss provisions / total lending

> ### Example
>
> Standard Chartered reports in 2014 loan loss provisions of 4,073 Mio. US-$ (Annual report 2014, p. 275). Loans and advances to banks are 83,890 Mio. US-$ (31.12.2013: 83,702 Mio. US-$), loans and advances to customers are 284,695 Mio. US-$ (31.12.2013: 290,708 Mio. US-$) (Annual report 2014, p. 227).
>
> Average total lending is: (83,890 + 83,702 + 282,695 + 290,708) / 2 = 371,498
>
> The provision cover ratio is:
>
> provision cover ratio = 4,073 / 370,498 = 1.10%

The provision cover ratio should be sufficiently high to cover defaults for the coming years without the necessity of additional loan loss provisions. For this, we can calculate the following ratio:

duration of loan loss provisions = total loan loss provisions / average defaults

At this stage, we have only the defaults of 2014, so we use this to calculate the duration of loan loss provisions.

> ### Example
>
> Standard Chartered reports in 2014 loan loss provisions of 4,073 Mio. US-$ (Annual report 2014, p. 275). Additionally, it reports the following data:

Loan loss provisions from the year before	3,547 (Annual report 2013, pp. 276, 277)
Net loan loss provision	2,141 (Annual report 2014, p. 225)
Loan loss provisions of this year	4,073 (Annual report 2014, p. 275)

utilisation = loan loss provisions from the year before + net loan loss provision − loan loss provisions of this year

utilisation = 3,547 + 2,141 − 4,073 = 1,615

duration of loan loss provisions = 4,073 / 1,615 = 2.52 years

Example

Commerzbank reports in 2014 utilisation of loan loss provisions of 1,956 Mio. €. Loan loss provisions are 5,775 Mio. € (Annual report 2014, p. 203).

duration of loan loss provisions = 5,775 / 1,956 = 2.95 years

Example

BBVA reports in 2014 loan loss provisions of 14,273 Mio. US-$ (Annual report 2014, pp. 125, 126). Additionally it reports following data:

Loan loss provisions from the year before	14,990 (Annual report 2014, pp. 125, 126)
Net loan loss provision	4,304 (Annual report 2014, p. 7)
Loan loss provisions of this year	14,273 (Annual report 2014, p. 125, 126)

> utilisation = loan loss provisions from the year before + net loan loss provision – loan loss provisions of this year
>
> utilisation = 14,990 + 4,304 − 14,273 = 5,021
>
> duration of loan loss provisions = 14,273 / 5,021 = 2.84 years

As we can see, the difference in the duration of loan loss provisions is not very big between these three banks. Standard Chartered has a slightly shorter duration than the other two banks.

What value should the duration of loan loss provisions have? A high value can say two different things:

1. A very conservative accounting policy for impairments – so hidden reserves can be assumed to be in the loan loss provisions.
2. A bad credit portfolio, so the loan loss provisions will really be needed in the future. This means a higher default rate in the near future.

On the other hand, a low value can say:

1. A very good credit portfolio, which means that the default rate will go down in the near future.
2. Too little loan loss provisions, so with a constant default rate higher loan loss provisions will have to be made in the near future.

For the external analysis, we need comparable data. If one bank has a duration of loan loss provisions of two years and another bank has five years, the first bank has a higher equity perhaps only because its risk policy is not appropriate. In the analysis we have to make them comparable. The right approach is to increase the loan loss provisions from the first bank so that its duration is also five years for the purposes of the analysis.

5.4 Interest income

5.4.1 Interest income margin

The interest income margin shows the return on the assets which produce interest.

interest income margin = interest income / (loans and receivables + debt securities)

It is important not to use the total assets as the denominator. Total assets include financial assets held for trading, for example – these assets do not produce interest income but trading income. Only in cases where a bank's total assets are almost entirely comprised of loans and receivables and debt securities should total assets be used.

Example

UniCredit reports the following data (Annual report 2014, pp. 88, 90, 190, 191, 192, 193, 252):

Debt securities in available-for-sale financial assets	94,226 Mio. €
Debt securities in held-to-maturity financial assets	2,617 Mio. €
Loans and receivables with banks	68,730 Mio. €
Loans and receivables with customers	470,569 Mio. €
Interest income	18,524 Mio. €

In interest income, only interest income from debt securities in AfS (available-for-sale), HtM (held-to-maturity), and loans and receivables are included.

interest income margin = 18,524 / 636,142 = 2.91%

The interest income margin can be compared between banks, but it only makes sense if the banks compared conduct business in the same geographical area. Different areas generally have different interest rates, so a bank like HSBC should have at the moment a higher interest income margin than UniCredit, for example, because in Asia the interest rates are mostly higher than in Europe, where UniCredit is doing its business.

Additionally, the interest income margin alone is not as important as the net interest margin. To calculate the net interest margin, we first need the interest expenses margin.

5.4.2 Interest expenses margin

The interest expenses margin shows how high the costs are for those liabilities which cost interest.

interest expenses margin = interest expenses / (deposits + debt securities in issue)

It is important not to use the total liabilities as the denominator. Like total assets, total liabilities include financial liabilities held for trading. Only in cases where a bank's total liabilities are comprised almost entirely of deposits and debt securities should total liabilities be used.

Example

UniCredit reports the following data (Annual report 2014, pp. 88, 90, 190, 191, 192, 193, 252):

Deposits from banks	106,037 Mio. €
Deposits from customers	410,412 Mio. €
Debt securities in issue	150,276 Mio. €
Interest expenses	8,373 Mio. €

> In interest expenses, only interest expenses from debt securities in issue and deposits are included.
>
> interest expenses margin = 8,373 / 666,725 = 1.26%

What was said for the interest income margin applies also to the interest expenses margin. We need the net interest income margin to be able to interpret it.

5.4.3 Net interest income margin

After calculating interest income margin and interest expenses margin, net interest income margin is easy to calculate:

net interest income margin = interest income margin – interest expenses margin

> ### Example
>
> For UniCredit we calculated above as follows:
>
> interest income margin = 18,524 / 636,142 = 2.91%
>
> interest expenses margin = 8,373 / 666,725 = 1.26%
>
> net interest income margin = 2.91% – 1.26% = 1.65%

The net interest income margin can be compared between different banks.

> ### Note
>
> In their notes, banks tend to divide up their asset positions in different ways. We have to look carefully at what should be included in the ratios and what should not.

Example

HSBC reports the following data (Annual report 2014, pp. 335, 337, 399):

Treasury and other eligible bills	81,517 Mio. US-$
Debt securities	323,256 Mio. US-$
Reverse repurchase agreements	161,713 Mio. US-$
Hong Kong Government certificates of indebtedness	27,674 Mio. US-$
Loans and receivables with banks	112,149 Mio. US-$
Loans and receivables with customers	974,660 Mio. US-$
Interest income	50,955 Mio. US-$

In interest income, only interest income from debt securities in AfS, HtM, and loans and receivables is included.

interest income margin = 50,955 / 1,680,969 = 3.03%

Deposits by banks	$77,426 Mio. US-$
Customers accounts	1,350,642 Mio. US-$
Repurchase agreements	107,432 Mio. US-$
Debt securities in issue	95,947 Mio. US-$
Interest expenses	16,250 Mio. US-$

interest expenses margin = 16,250 / 1,631,447 = 1.00%

net interest income margin = 3.03% − 1.00% = 2.03%

The net interest income margin of HSBC is higher than for UniCredit.

The net interest income margin alone has no great meaning. The higher the credit risks a bank takes, the higher the net interest income margin will be. The net interest income margin after risk costs is calculated as follows:

net interest income margin after risk costs = net interest income margin – default rate or allocation rate

Example

Standard Chartered reports the following data (Annual report 2014, pp. 225, 227, 278):

Debt securities	77,942 Mio. US-$
Loans and receivables with banks	83,890 Mio. US-$
Loans and receivables with customers	284,695 Mio. US-$
Interest income	16,984 Mio. US-$

interest income margin = 16,984 / 446,527 = 3.80%

Deposits by banks	54,391 Mio. US-$
Customer accounts	405,353 Mio. US-$
Debt securities in issue	71,951 Mio. US-$
Interest expenses	5,981 Mio. US-$

interest expenses margin = 5,981 / 531,695 = 1.12%

net interest income margin = 3.80% – 1.12% = 2.68%

Standard Chartered reports the following data:

Loan loss provisions from the year before	3,547 (Annual report 2013, pp. 276, 277)
Net loan loss provision	2,141 (Annual report 2014, p. 225)
Loan loss provisions of this year	4,073 (Annual report 2014, p. 275)

utilisation = loan loss provisions from the year before + net loan loss provision – loan loss provisions of this year

utilisation = 3,547 + 2,141 – 4,073 = 1,615

Loans and advances to banks are 83,890 Mio. US-$ (31.12.2013: 83,702 Mio. US-$), loans and advances to customers are 284,695 Mio. US-$ (31.12.2013: 290,708 Mio. US-$) (Annual report 2014, p. 227).

Average total lending is: (83,890 + 83,702 + 284,695 + 290,708) / 2 = 371,498

The default ratio is:

default ratio = 1,615 / 371,498 = 0.43%

net interest income margin after risk costs = 2.68% – 0.43% = 2.25%

Standard Chartered is definitely in a better position than UniCredit and HSBC because the net interest income margin after risk costs is higher than their net interest income margin *before* risk costs.

HSBC reports its own allocation ratio as 0.43% (Annual report 2014, p. 142). So its net interest income margin after risk costs is 2.03% – 0.43% = 1.60%.

A higher net interest income margin may not always be better if too high credit risks are involved. A higher net interest income margin after risk costs is always better, because a bank can achieve higher margin *after* risk costs.

A bank with low net interest income margin after risk costs is more likely to get into problems in a recession or a financial crisis than a bank with high net interest income margin after risk costs.

Example

If the default rate of Standard Chartered doubles or triples in a recession, the net interest income margin after risk costs is still 1.82% or 1.39% respectively. Even in these cases, the bank has no risk of failure because of its credit risks.

Net interest income margin after risk costs – together with net fee income and net trading income – must be high enough to finance operating expenses. It is better to achieve this only with net fee income, because the financial crisis has shown that net trading income can produce high losses. A bank should have 1.50% net interest income margin after risk costs as a minimum. If it has less, it has a higher possibility of getting into problems in a crisis.

Example

Commerzbank reports the following data (Annual report 2014, pp. 147, 150, 184, 278):

Debt securities	89,076 Mio. €
Claims on banks	80,036 Mio. €
Claims on customers	232,867 Mio. €
Interest income	10,323 Mio. €

interest income margin = 10,323 / 401,979 = 2.57%

Liabilities to banks	99,443 Mio. €
Liabilities to customers	248,977 Mio. €
Securitised liabilities	48,813 Mio. €
Interest expenses	4,987 Mio. €

interest expenses margin = 4,987 / 397,233 = 1.26%

net interest income margin = 2.57% – 1.26% = 1.31%

Commerzbank reports in 2014 utilisation of loan loss provisions of 1,956 Mio. € (Annual report 2014, p. 203). Loans and advances to banks are 80,036 Mio. € (31.12.2013: 87,545 Mio. €), loans and advances to customers are 232,867 Mio. € (31.12.2013: 245,938 Mio. €) (Annual report 2014, p. 337).

Average total lending is: (80,036 + 87,545 + 232,867 + 245,938) / 2 = 323,193

The default ratio is:

default ratio = 1,956 / 323,193 = 0.61%

net interest income margin after risk costs = 1.31% – 0.61% = 0.70%

Commerzbank only has a net interest income margin after risk costs of 0.70%. If the default ratio doubles in a recession or financial crisis, the margin is nearly 0%. Compared to Standard Chartered, Commerzbank has a much higher risk of getting into problems in a recession or financial crisis.

Even the net interest income margin after risks is not too meaningful on its own. It has to be compared with net fee margin and operating expenses to see if in a bad situation the bank will get losses immediately or if the margins are sufficiently high that a crisis would not wound the bank very much.

Note

Interest income and interest expenses from trading securities are reported by some banks in interest income and interest expenses. For analysis, we have to put them in trading income.

Example

Commerzbank (Annual report, p. 184):

Interest income (held for trading)	1,036 Mio. €
Interest expenses (held for trading)	130 Mio. €

5.5 Net fee income

The net fee income – or net commission income – is for most banks the second most important income source. For pure investment banks it is even the most important income source.

We can calculate a couple of different ratios for the net fee income:

importance of net fee income = net fee income / net operating income

The importance of net fee income shows which part of net operating income comes from net fee income.

Example

Commerzbank reports the following data (Annual report 2014, p. 147):

Net fee income	3,205 Mio. €
Net operating income	7,610 Mio. €

importance of net fee income = 3,205 / 7,610 = 42%

If we are trying to find the stability of bank income, net fee income is generally said to be more stable than net interest income. From that side, the higher importance of net fee income, the better the stability of bank net operating income.

Example

Net fee income of Deutsche Bank 2007-2014:

2007	12,289 Mio. €
2008	9,749 Mio. €
2009	8,911 Mio. €
2010	10,669 Mio. €
2011	11,544 Mio. €
2012	11,510 Mio. €
2013	12,308 Mio. €
2014	12,409 Mio. €

We can see that the net fee income of Deutsche Bank fell 25% in the financial crisis. Net interest income was as follows:

2007	8,849 Mio. €
2008	12,453 Mio. €
2009	12,459 Mio. €
2010	15,583 Mio. €

2011	17,445 Mio. €
2012	15,891 Mio. €
2013	14,834 Mio. €
2014	14,272 Mio. €

For Deutsche Bank, net interest income was the stable income base and net fee income the unstable one.

Whether net fee income is the stable part or net interest income is the stable part has to be checked from bank to bank. It depends mainly on the source of the net fee income.

Another common ratio to make the net fee income between banks comparable is the ratio of net fee income to total assets:

net fee margin = net fee income / total assets

Example

Standard Chartered reports the following data (Annual report 2014, pp. 225, 227):

Net fee income	4,179 Mio. €
Total assets	725,914 Mio. €

net fee margin = 4,179 / 725,914 = 0.58%

HSBC reports the following data (Annual report 2014, pp. 335, 337):

Net fee income	15,957 Mio. $
Total assets	2,634,139 Mio. $

net fee margin = 15,957 / 2,634,139 = 0.61%

Deutsche Bank reports the following data (Annual report 2014, pp. 349, 351):

Net fee income	12,409 Mio. €
Total assets	1,708,703 Mio. €

net fee margin = 12,409 / 1,708,703 = 0.73%

As we can see, net fee margin is highest for Deutsche Bank. It is a big investment bank, so this could have been expected.

HSBC and Standard Chartered, both more or less credit banks, have nearly the same margin.

Net fee income is more stable if the fee income comes from credit business rather than from investment banking.

Example

Net fee income of Commerzbank 2007-2014:

2007	3,150 Mio. €
2008	2,846 Mio. €
2009	3,722 Mio. €
2010	3,647 Mio. €
2011	3,495 Mio. €
2012	3,191 Mio. €
2013	3,215 Mio. €
2014	3,205 Mio. €

The net fee income of Commerzbank dropped only 10% in 2008 compared to 2007, while Deutsche Bank – with much more business in investment banking – lost 25% of its net income.

In fact, net interest income must be more stable than net fee income, because most of these earnings for the coming years are already saved through the credit contracts. Fee income has to be earned again and again.

5.6 Trading income

Trading income is the net income from trading with equity, securities or derivative products. It is the most volatile earnings source for a bank, which can be easily shown by the following example.

Example

Net trading income of Deutsche Bank 2007-2014:

Year	Net trading income
2007	7,175 Mio. €
2008	−9,992 Mio. €
2009	7,109 Mio. €
2010	3,354 Mio. €
2011	3,058 Mio. €
2012	5,599 Mio. €
2013	3,817 Mio. €
2014	4,299 Mio. €

Deutsche Bank's net trading income dropped significantly in 2008, making a loss in this position of nearly 10,000 Mio. €.

> Additionally, net trading income does not include operating expenses used to generate it. The real loss is therefore much higher.

As shown in section 5.4, some parts of trading income are presented in interest income for some banks. The reason is that there is interest income in trading positions too. Because IFRS has no rule for this topic, some banks show it in interest income and some in trading income.

To make banks comparable, all interest income and interest expenses due to trading positions have to be shown in the analysis in trading income.

5.7 Liquidity risk ratios

The measurement of liquidity risk is one of the goals of banking supervision. To achieve this, banking supervision uses a number of ratios from internal bank sources (for example, see Bank for International Settlements, Frequently Asked Questions on Basel III's January 2013 Liquidity Coverage Ratio framework, www.bis.org/publ/bcbs284.pdf).

For external analysis, we can only use the data provided in the financial statements. In fact, external analysis cannot give as good results as internal analysis. But because we do not have the same sources as banking supervision, we can only use the second-best data.

5.7.1 Interbank ratio

The interbank ratio shows the ratio of claims on banks to deposits from banks:

interbank ratio = claims on banks / deposits from banks

The interbank ratio is a measure of the liquidity risk of a bank. While deposits from customers are said to be very stable even in a crisis, deposits from banks can be lost very quickly, as seen in the world financial crisis. Because of this, an interbank ratio of more than 100% is said to be a good sign for liquidity risk.

The interbank ratio can be calculated very easily directly from the data in the balance sheet.

Example

HSBC reports the following data (Annual report 2014, p. 337):

Loans and advances to banks	112,149
Deposits by banks	77,426

interbank ratio = 112,149 / 77,426 = 144.8%

Example

Commerzbank reports the following data (Annual report 2014, p. 150):

Loans and advances to banks	80,036
Deposits by banks	99,443

interbank ratio = 80,036 / 99,443 = 80.5%

While HSBC is far above 100%, Commerzbank reaches only 80.5%. So – following the interbank ratio – Commerzbank is the more risky bank. Unfortunately, it is not that easy to measure the liquidity risk of a bank.

First of all, the maturity of loans and deposits has to be included. If all claims on banks are long term and all deposits by banks are short term, a high interbank ratio has no meaning. Banks have to publish the maturity of the assets and liabilities in the notes, so this information can be used to calculate the interbank ratio for different maturities.

short-term interbank ratio = short-term claims on banks / short-term deposits from banks

Example

HSBC reports the following data (Annual report 2014, pp. 427, 428):

Loans and advances to banks due not more than 1 month	73,758
Deposits by banks due not more than 1 month	66,829

short-term interbank ratio = 73,758 / 66,829 = 110.4%

Example

Commerzbank reports the following data (Annual report 2014, p. 246):

Claims on banks due on demand and unlimited term	29,070
Liabilities to banks due on demand and unlimited term	43,629

short-term interbank ratio = 29,070 / 43,629 = 66.6%

For both banks, the short-term interbank ratio is much lower than the interbank ratio. The reason is that there are many more longer-term loans than longer-term liabilities for these banks. HSBC still has a ratio above 100%, while Commerzbank is well under 100%. This is – following the interpretation of the ratio – a sign of high liquidity risk.

A second problem when measuring the liquidity risk is that we do not know about unused credit lines that a bank may have from other banks.

Third, if banks are able to get easy money from a central bank, the interbank ratio is no longer a sign of liquidity risk.

A final point to consider is that all loans to banks and deposits by banks of all banks worldwide have to be equal when summed. Around half of banks have an interbank ratio over 100%, the other half under 100%. This would suggest that around one half of all banks have high liquidity risk. This, in fact, makes no sense. The effect would be that around half of all banks would be analysed with high liquidity risk and the other half without liquidity risk.

5.7.2 Deposit run-off ratio

The deposit run-off ratio shows the percentage of cash reserve and short-term assets to short-term liabilities.

deposit run-off ratio = (cash reserve + short-term assets) / short-term liabilities

Example

Commerzbank reports the following data (Annual report 2014, pp. 150, 246):

Cash reserve	4,897
Short-term assets (Assets due on demand and unlimited term)	55,555
Short-term liabilities (Liabilities due on demand and unlimited term)	195,357

deposit run-off ratio = (4,897 + 55,555) / 195,357 = 30.9%

Example

HSBC reports the following data (Annual report 2014, pp. 427, 428):

Short-term assets (Assets due not more than 1 month)	1,246,820
Short-term liabilities (Liabilities due not more than 1 month)	1,940,522

deposit run-off ratio = 1,246,820 / 1,940,522 = 64.3%

HSBC has a much higher deposit run-off ratio than Commerzbank. Commerzbank could pay back only 31% of all short-term liabilities with its cash reserves and short-term assets. This may sound very low, but in fact most parts of short-term liabilities are legally short term, but in reality long term, because it can be assumed that all customers will not take back all of their money simultaneously.

Following the deposit base theory, a portion of short-term liabilities are permanently available for a bank. Even in a bank run, not all short-term liabilities have to be paid back immediately. The question is, what percentage of short-term liabilities has to be in cash or what percentage of short-term assets has to be held to have enough liquidity in a crisis.

Regional markets differ in the deposit base a bank can calculate as permanent. Because of this, it is hard to define the threshold a bank should be above in the deposit run-off ratio. In the European Union there is a deposit guarantee, so customers will not take back their money as quickly as in countries without a deposit guarantee.

In fact, the much higher deposit run-off ratio of HSBC may be due to the markets HSBC is working in. While Commerzbank mostly does business in the countries of the European Union, HSBC is active worldwide. A higher deposit run-off ratio is therefore more of a requirement for HSBC than it is for Commerzbank.

5.8 Credit ratios

We can calculate different ratios for the credit business of a bank.

5.8.1 Loan-to-deposit ratio

The loan-to-deposit ratio shows the relation of the loans to customers to the deposits by customers:

loan-to-deposit ratio = loans to customers / deposits by customers

It shows if a bank can refinance its total loans with its own deposits or if it has to take money from other banks to refinance the loans. From a liquidity risk view, the loan-to-deposit ratio should be under 100%.

Example

HSBC reports the following data (Annual report 2014, p. 337):

Loans to customers	974,660
Customer accounts	1,350,642

loan-to-deposit ratio = 974,660 / 1,350,642 = 72.2%

Example

Commerzbank reports the following data (Annual report 2014, pp. 150, 151):

Claims on customers	232,867
Liabilities to customers	248,977

loan-to-deposit ratio = 232,867 / 248,977 = 93.5%

Both Commerzbank and HSBC have a ratio under 100%. HSBC can use a large amount from customer accounts to refinance financial investments, which were 415 billion US-$ in 2014 (Annual report, 2014, p. 337).

By comparison, Commerzbank has to refinance its financial investments not only with customer accounts, but also liabilities to banks and securitised liabilities.

The loan-to-deposit ratio is easy to understand, but it has disadvantages. It does not show the maturity of loans and liabilities, so even a ratio under 100% can come with a high liquidity risk if there is significant maturity transformation.

5.8.2 Short-term loan-to-deposit ratio

Additionally, we can calculate a loan-to-deposit ratio for short maturities only:

short-term loan-to-deposit ratio = short-term loans to customers / short-term deposits by customers

Example

HSBC reports the following data (Annual report 2014, p. 337):

Loans to customers due not more than 1 month	230,736
Customer accounts due not more than 1 month	1,229,694

short-term loan-to-deposit ratio = 230,736 / 1,229,694 = 18.8%

This quote shows for HSBC that even though 72% of customer loans were used for loans to customers, only 18.8% of short-term customer loans were used for short-term loans to customers. In fact, HSBC is using a huge maturity transformation. This would lead to high losses in the case of an inverted maturity structure.

6. Analysis of the Profit and Loss Account

In the last chapter we looked at several ratios which can be used to analyse banks, but none of them is good enough to provide a quick impression about a bank.

In this chapter, we will focus on the profit and loss account and try to calculate an operating income for each bank. Operating income is that part of the profit which can be repeated in the following periods. All extraordinary incomes and expenses are not part of the operating income.

As mentioned previously, this is much easier to calculate for a bank than for a non-bank, because we already know that a high percentage of assets and liabilities has a rest-duration of more than one year or even much longer.

To analyse the profit and loss account, we need the profit and loss account itself and its notes. How much is mentioned in the notes depends on the bank itself and to a degree the country it comes from. IFRS is the same for all countries that use it, but sometimes the standards are applied differently. Some banks give plenty of information in the notes, some banks give only a minimum.

In financial statement analysis, we act in the opposite way to a court of law: if we are in doubt, we are against the bank. This means that if a bank does not give enough information in the notes, in doubt we will put income in extraordinary income and expenses in operating income!

This is the only way to force banks to give the kind of information we need for the analysis (as non-banks do).

The profit and loss account of a bank following IFRS normally contains the following positions:

- Interest income
- Interest expense
- Cost of risk
- Commission income
- Commission expense
- Trading income
- Net income from other activities
- Salaries
- Other operating expenses
- Depreciation, amortisation and impairments
- Income tax

In the following sections, an analysis of these positions is presented for all of the banks mentioned in the book. First the original profit and loss account of each bank is mentioned. After the reclassifications have been made, amounts are put into other accounts than those used originally by the bank.

6.1 Banca Carige

Banca Carige published the following data from its profit and loss account (Annual report 2014, p. 81):

Position	Amount (€m)
Interest income	795
Interest expense	442

Position	Amount (€m)
Cost of risk	−652
Net interest income after cost of risk	−309
Commission income	296
Commission expense	51
Net commission income	245
Trading income	5
Net income from other activities	47
Salaries	412
Other operating expenses	249
Depreciation, amortisation and impairments	21
Income before tax	−579
Income tax	−171
Income after tax	−408
Income from discontinued operations after tax	−139
Net income	−547

We have to make the following reclassifications:

- In interest income Banca Carige has included interest income from financial assets held for trading of 15 Mio. €. This has to be reclassified to trading income.

- In net income from other activities there is net profit from hedging activities of 2 Mio. €. This originally comes from interest income so it has to be reclassified to interest income.

- In net income from other activities there are profits and losses on disposals/repurchases of 90 Mio. €. This is one-time income and has to be reclassified to extraordinary income.

- In net income from other activities there are profits/losses on financial assets and liabilities designated at fair value of −21 Mio. €.

This originally comes from interest income so it has to be reclassified to interest expenses.

- All other amounts in the net income from other activities are extraordinary because they come from non-banking-activities like rental income.

- Income from discontinued operations after tax is extraordinary.

Position	Amount (€m)
Interest income	782
Interest expense	463
Cost of risk	−652
Net interest income after cost of risk	−333
Commission income	296
Commission expense	51
Net commission income	245
Trading income	20
Salaries	412
Other operating expenses	249
Depreciation, amortisation and impairments	21
Income before tax	−654
Income tax	−171
Income after tax	−408
Net income	−547
Extraordinary income	−73

The net income of Banca Carige is strongly negative. The main reason for this is the very high cost of risk of 652 Mio. €. Unfortunately, Banca Carige does not give enough information in the notes to enable us to analyse the cost of risk further, but we can say that this amount is much too high for operating income. The cost of risk has to fall strongly in the near future, but it is not possible to calculate what amount to expect. For that we need information like the allocation or default ratio (section 5.3).

Without considering the cost of risk, Banca Carige already has a negative income before tax of −2 Mio. €. The cost of risk is from that side *only* an additional loss. In fact, Banca Carige has too little earnings just as it has too high costs. In its current condition, it cannot survive.

With risk-weighted assets of 20,474 Mio. € (Annual report 2014, p. 371), Banca Carige has a RoRWA of −547 / 20,474 = −2.67%.

6.2 Banca Monte dei Paschi

Banca Monte dei Paschi published the following data from its profit and loss account (Annual report 2014, p. 124):

Position	Amount (€m)
Interest income	5,213
Interest expense	3,079
Cost of risk	−7,821
Net interest income after cost of risk	−5,687
Commission income	2,087
Commission expense	389
Net commission income	1,698
Trading income	81
Net income from other activities	−247
Salaries	2,052
Other operating expenses	1,168
Depreciation, amortisation and impairments	307

Position	Amount (€m)
Income before tax	−7,684
Income tax	−2,336
Income after tax	−5,347
Income from discontinued operations after tax	0
Net Income	−5,347

We have to make the following reclassifications:

- In interest income Banca Monte dei Paschi has included interest income from financial assets held for trading of 162 Mio. €. This has to be reclassified to trading income. The same for interest expenses of 12 Mio. €.

- In net income from other activities there is dividends and similar income of +37 Mio. €. This has to be reclassified to interest income.

- In net income from other activities there is net profit from hedging activities of −16 Mio. €. This originally comes from interest expenses so it has to be reclassified to interest expenses.

- In net income from other activities there are profits and losses on disposals/repurchases of 159 Mio. €. This is one-time income and has to be reclassified to extraordinary income.

- In net income from other activities there are profits/losses on financial assets and liabilities designated at fair value of +2 Mio. €. This originally comes from interest income so it has to be reclassified to interest expenses.

- In net income from other activities there are net provisions for risks and charges of −177 Mio. €. This originally comes from operating business so it has to be reclassified to other operating expenses.

- All other amounts in the net income from other activities are extraordinary because they come from non-banking activities like rental income.

- Income from discontinued operations after tax is extraordinary.

Position	Amount (€m)
Interest income	5,090
Interest expense	3,083
Cost of risk	−7,821
Net interest income after cost of risk	−5,851
Commission income	2,087
Commission expense	389
Net commission income	1,698
Trading income	231
Salaries	2,052
Other operating expenses	1,345
Depreciation, amortisation and impairments	307
Income before tax	−7,591
Income tax	−2,336
Income after tax	−5,254
Income from discontinued operations after tax	0
Net income	−5,254
Extraordinary income	−93

The net income of Banca Monte dei Paschi is strongly negative. The main reason for this is the very high cost of risk of 7,821 Mio. €. Unfortunately, this bank does not give enough information in the notes to further analyse the cost of risk, but we can say that this amount is much too high for operating income. The cost of risk will have to fall strongly in the near future, but it is not possible to calculate what amount to expect. For that we need information like the allocation or default ratio (section 5.3).

Banca Monte dei Paschi is mainly dependent on the cost of risk. Without this, the bank would be lightly profitable. This is still not enough to be called healthy, because its operating expenses have to be reduced.

It has to be said that Banca Monte de Paschi is far from a healthy bank. We will see in the near future if it is able to turn the situation around.

With risk-weighted assets of 76,220 Mio. € (Annual report 2014, p. 476), Banca Monte dei Paschi has a RoRWA of −5,254 / 76,220 = −6.89%.

6.3 Banco Bilbao Vizcaya Argentaria

Banco Bilbao Vizcaya Argentaria (BBVA) published the following data from its profit and loss account (Annual report 2014, pp. 7–8):

Position	Amount (€m)
Interest income	22,838
Interest expense	8,456
Cost of risk	−4,304
Net interest income after cost of risk	10,078
Commission income	5,530
Commission expense	1,356
Net commission income	4,174
Trading income	11
Net income from other activities	276
Salaries	5,410
Other operating expenses	4,004
Depreciation, amortisation and impairments	1,145
Income before tax	3,980
Income tax	898
Income after tax	3,082

Position	Amount (€m)
Income from discontinued operations after tax	0
Net income	3,082

We have to make the following reclassifications:

- In interest income BBVA includes interest income from financial assets held for trading of 1,134 Mio. €. This has to be reclassified to trading income.

- In net income from other activities there is dividend income of +531 Mio. €. This has to be reclassified to interest income.

- In net income from other activities there is a share of profit or loss of entities accounted for using the equity method of 343 Mio. €. This does not originate from bank business (e.g. share of Telefonica), so we put it in the extraordinary income.

- In net income from other activities there are net gains on financial assets and liabilities of 1,435 Mio. €. This is one-time income and has to be reclassified to extraordinary income.

- In net income from other activities there are exchange differences of +699 Mio. €. This is one-time income so it has to be reclassified to extraordinary income.

- In net income from other activities there are other operating income and expenses of +4,581 Mio. € and −5,420 Mio. €. Within this is included the income and expenses from insurance and reinsurance contracts (+3,622 Mio. € and −2,714 Mio. €) and financial income from non-financial services of 650 Mio. €. This is operating income. The rest of this position is extraordinary.

- In net income from other activities there are provisions of −1,142 Mio. €. These are operating expenses.

- All other amounts in the net income from other activities are extraordinary because they come from non-banking activities like rental income.

- Unlike Banca Carige and Banca Monte dei Paschi, BBVA gives information about the cost of risk (Annual report 2014, p. 86). In 2014, the cost of risk following the income statement is 4,304 Mio. €. The transfers to written-off loans are 4,464 Mio. €. With total loans and receivables of 372,375 Mio. € (31.12.2014) and 350,945 Mio. € (31.12.2013) (Annual report 2014, p. 4), we get an allocation ratio of 4,304 / ((372,375 + 350,945) / 2) = 1.19% and a default ratio of 4,464 / ((372,375 + 350,945) / 2) = 1.23%. For 2013, the allocation ratio is 1.54% and the default rate is 1.02%. For a more detailed analysis we should use more data, maybe from the last ten years or even longer.

Position	Amount (€m)
Interest income	22,235
Interest expense	8,456
Cost of risk	−4,304
Net interest income after cost of risk	9,475
Commission income	5,530
Commission expense	1,356
Net commission income	4,174
Trading income	1,145
Other operating income	1,558
Salaries	5,410
Other operating expenses	5,146
Depreciation, amortisation and impairments	1,145
Income before tax	4,651
Income tax	898
Income after tax	3,753
Income from discontinued operations after tax	0
Net income	3,753
Extraordinary income	−671

The net income of BBVA is strongly positive. As a healthy bank, BBVA has only low trading income, but the main income sources are interest and commission income.

With risk-weighted assets of 637,572 Mio. € (Annual report 2014, p. 174), BBVA has a RoRWA of 3,753 / 637,572 = 0.59%.

6.4 Banco Comercial Portugues

Banco Comercial Portugues published the following data from its profit and loss account (Annual report 2014, p. 152):

Position	Amount (€m)
Interest income	2,653
Interest expense	1,536
Cost of risk	−1,107
Net interest income after cost of risk	9
Commission income	812
Commission expense	131
Net commission income	681
Trading income	154
Net income from other activities	132
Salaries	636
Other operating expenses	448
Depreciation, amortisation and impairments	66
Income before tax	−173
Income tax	−98
Income after tax	−76
Income from discontinued operations after tax	−41
Net income	−117

We have to make the following reclassifications:

- In interest income Banco Comercial Portugues has included interest income from financial assets held for trading of +17 Mio. €. This has to be reclassified to trading income.

- In net income from other activities there is dividend income of +6 Mio. €. This has to be reclassified to interest income.

- In net income from other activities there are net gains/losses from financial assets of 288 Mio. €. This is originally extraordinary income.

- In net income from other activities there is other operating income of -53 Mio. €. This is originally operating expenses.

- In net income from other activities there is net income from non-bank activities of +19 Mio. €. This is one-time income so it has to be reclassified to extraordinary income.

- In net income from other activities there are impairments of −128 Mio. €. This is originally extraordinary income.

- In net income from other activities there are provisions of −81 Mio. €. These are originally operating expenses.

- All other amounts in the net income from other activities are extraordinary because they come from non-banking activities like rental income.

- Banco Comercial Portugues publishes the impairment for credit risk at a total of 3,483 Mio. € for 2014 and 3,420 Mio. € for 2013 (Annual report 2014, p. 187), so it increased by 63 Mio. €. While the loans impairments were 1,107 Mio. € in 2014 (Annual report 2014, p. 183), the default must have been 1,107 Mio. € − 63 Mio. € = 1,044 Mio. €.

Position	(€m)
Interest income	2,642
Interest expense	1,536
Cost of risk	−1,107

Position	(€m)
Net interest income after cost of risk	−1
Commission income	812
Commission expense	131
Net commission income	681
Trading income	171
Salaries	636
Other operating expenses	582
Depreciation, amortisation and impairments	66
Income before tax	−433
Income tax	-98
Income after tax	−335
Income from discontinued operations after tax	-41
Net income	−377
Net income from other activities	260

Banco Comercial Portugues has a strongly negative income. This comes from the very high cost of risk. With defaults of 1,044 Mio. € and loans of 53,686 Mio. €, the default ratio is 1.94%, which is much too high for a bank like Banco Comercial Portugues. The net interest income after cost of risk is negative. Normally for this kind of bank, the net interest income after the cost of risk should be double the net commission income, so around 1,350 Mio. €. This is not possible because the cost of risk is only 1,107 Mio. €. So Banco Comercial Portugues has both a cost of risk problem and also a too-low interest income problem.

With risk-weighted assets of 42,376 Mio. € (Annual report 2014, p. 295), Banco Comercial Portugues has a RoRWA of −335 / 42,376 = −0.79%.

Banco Comercial Portugues has to strengthen its credit portfolio. If it is able to get the cost of risk to a *normal* amount of 200-300 Mio. €, it will be profitable again, but even then only with a RoRWA of 1.1%.

The market Banco Comercial Portugues is working in – the Portuguese market – seems not to provide the kind of profits that a bank should be able to generate.

6.5 Banco de Sabadell

Banco de Sabadell published the following data from its profit and loss account (Annual report 2014, p. 135):

Position	Amount (€m)
Interest income	4,513
Interest expense	2,254
Cost of risk	−1,764
Net interest income after cost of risk	495
Commission income	971
Commission expense	110
Net commission income	861
Trading income	1,764
Net income from other activities	−593
Salaries	1,203
Other operating expenses	571
Depreciation, amortisation and impairments	278
Income before tax	486
Income tax	110
Income after tax	377
Income from discontinued operations after tax	0
Net income	377

We have to make the following reclassifications:

- In net income from other activities there is dividend income of +9 Mio. €. This has to be reclassified to interest income.

- In net income from other activities there are exchange differences of +100 Mio. €. This was originally extraordinary income.

- In net income from other activities there are income and expenses from insurance and reinsurance contracts of +256 and −307 Mio. €. This was originally operating income.

- In net income from other activities there are provisions of +170 Mio. €. This is one-time income so it has to be reclassified to extraordinary income.

- In net income from other activities there are impairments of −452 Mio. €. This was originally extraordinary income.

- In net income from other activities there are gains/losses from non-current assets held for sale of −439 Mio. €. This was originally extraordinary income.

- In net income from other activities there are other operating expenses from contribution to deposit guarantee funds of −158 Mio. €. This was originally operating expenses.

- All other amounts in the net income from other activities are extraordinary because they come from non-bank activities like rental income.

- Banco de Sabadell publishes the utilisation of allowances of 2,182 Mio. € for 2014 and 708 Mio. € for 2013 (Annual report 2014, p. 191), while the loans impairments were 1,764 Mio. € in 2014 (Annual report 2014, p. 135).

Position	Amount (€m)
Interest income	4,522
Interest expense	2,254
Cost of risk	−1,764
Net interest income after cost of risk	504

Position	Amount (€m)
Commission income	971
Commission expense	110
Net commission income	861
Trading income	1,764
Operating income from insurance activities	–51
Salaries	1,203
Other operating expenses	729
Depreciation, amortisation and impairments	278
Income before tax	879
Income tax	110
Income after tax	770
Income from discontinued operations after tax	0
Net income	770
Net income from other activities	–393

At first view, Banco de Sabadell is profitable. With risk-weighted assets of 60,071 Mio. € (Annual report 2014, p. 101), it has a RoRWA of 770 / 60,071 = 1.28%, which is high compared to other banks.

This profit appears very high at first, but it comes from a one-time effect. 1,861 Mio. € profit was generated through selling debt securities (Annual report 2014, p. 260). Without this, Banco de Sabadell is highly unprofitable. For the purposes of the analysis this profit has to be eliminated, so the real net income is -1,091 Mio. € and the real RoRWA = −1,091 / 60,071 = −1.82%.

The origin of this high deficit is the high cost of risk. The allocation ratio for 2014 is 1,764 / 117,895 = 1.50% and the default ratio is 2,182 / 117,895 = 1.85%. Ratios of 0.50% would be normal for this kind of bank, and in this case the cost of risk would fall to 589 Mio. €, which means an increase of 1,175 Mio. € in income before tax. Net income would then be lightly positive, at 84 Mio. €, which is still much too little for a bank like Banco de Sabadell.

In fact, we have to expect net interest income after cost of risk of double the net commission income, so around 1,700 Mio. €, which would be reached with an allocation ratio of 0.50%. It seems like Banco de Sabadell has a problem on the cost side.

6.6 Banco Popolare

Banco Popolare published the following data from its profit and loss account (Annual report 2014, p. 167):

Position	Amount (€m)
Interest income	3,263
Interest expense	1,706
Cost of risk	−3,476
Net interest income after cost of risk	−1,920
Commission income	1,481
Commission expense	96
Net commission income	1,385
Trading income	138
Net income from other activities	128
Salaries	1,423
Other operating expenses	858
Depreciation, amortisation and impairments	252
Income before tax	−2,800
Income tax	−815
Income after tax	−1,985

Position	Amount (€m)
Income from discontinued operations after tax	0
Net income	−1,985

We have to make the following reclassifications:

- In interest income Banco Popolare has included interest income from financial assets held for trading of +291 Mio. € and interest expenses of −3 Mio. €. This has to be reclassified to trading income.

- In net income from other activities there is dividend income of +35 Mio. €. This has to be reclassified to interest income.

- In net income from other activities there are fair value adjustments in hedge accounting of −7 Mio. €. This was originally interest expenses.

- In net income from other activities there are profits/losses on disposal or repurchase of +40 Mio. €. This was originally extraordinary income.

- In net income from other activities there are profits/losses on financial assets and liabilities designated at fair value of −46 Mio. €. This is one-time income so it has to be reclassified to extraordinary income.

- In net income from other activities there are impairments of −110 Mio. €. This was originally extraordinary income.

- In net income from other activities there are other operating income of +363 Mio. €. This was originally extraordinary income.

- All other amounts in the net income from other activities are extraordinary because they come from non-banking activities like rental income.

- Banco Popolare publishes the utilisation of allowances of 2,182 Mio. € for 2014 and 708 Mio. € for 2013 (Annual report 2014, p. 191), while the loans impairments were 1,764 Mio. € in 2014 (Annual report 2014, p. 135).

Position	Amount (€m)
Interest income	3,007
Interest expense	1,710
Cost of risk	–3,476
Net interest income after cost of risk	–2,180
Commission income	1,481
Commission expense	96
Net commission income	1,385
Trading income	426
Salaries	1,423
Other operating expenses	858
Depreciation, amortisation and impairments	252
Income before tax	–2,900
Income tax	-815
Income after tax	–2,085
Income from discontinued operations after tax	0
Net income	–2,085
Net income from other activities	100

Banco Popolare is highly unprofitable. This is mostly due to the extremely high cost of risk, which makes the net interest income after the cost of risk highly negative. Unfortunately, Banco Popolare does not give enough information in the notes to further analyse the cost of risk, but we can say that this amount is much too high for operating income. The cost of risk has to fall strongly in the near future, but it is not possible to calculate what amount to expect. For that we need information like the allocation or default ratio (section 5.3).

An expected allocation ratio of 0.5% would lead to cost of risk of 79,824 Mio. € (Loans to customers, Annual report 2014, p. 166) × 0.5%

= 399 Mio. €. With this amount, Banco Popolare would reach a net income of +992 Mio. €!

With risk-weighted assets of 47,987 Mio. € (Annual report 2014, p. 391), it has a RoRWA of −2,085 / 47,987 = −4.34%.

6.7 Banco Popular

Banco Popular published the following data from its profit and loss account (Annual report 2014, p. 167):

Position	Amount (€m)
Interest income	4,167
Interest expense	1,836
Cost of risk	−1,691
Net interest income after cost of risk	640
Commission income	739
Commission expense	85
Net commission income	654
Trading income	821
Net income from other activities	-23
Salaries	946
Other operating expenses	780
Depreciation, amortisation and impairments	145
Income before tax	373
Income tax	43
Income after tax	330
Income from discontinued operations after tax	0
Net income	330

We have to make the following reclassifications:

- In net income from other activities there is the dividend income of +14 Mio. €. This has to be reclassified to interest income.

- In net income from other activities there is a share of profits of associated companies of +33 Mio. €. This is not originally banking business and therefore it is extraordinary income.

- In net income from other activities there are exchange differences of +47 Mio. €. This is originally extraordinary income.

- In net income from other activities there are provisioning expenses of −45 Mio. €. This is operating expenses.

- In net income from other activities there are impairments of −110 Mio. €. This is originally extraordinary income.

- In net income from other activities there are other impairment losses of −48 Mio. €. This is originally extraordinary income.

- In net income from other activities there are gains/losses on disposal of assets of +498 Mio. €. This is originally extraordinary income.

- The same is true for gains/losses on non-current assets of −496 Mio. €. Impairment losses of 444 Mio. € are included here. It can be argued that these losses are nothing other than the cost of risk for securities. In that case we would have to use them in the cost of risk too. In this book we treat them as extraordinary, but both methods are possible.

- In net income from other activities there are contributions to guarantee funds (Annual report 2014, p. 454) of 116 Mio. €. This is an operating expense.

- All other amounts in the net income from other activities are extraordinary because they come from non-banking activities like rental income.

- Banco Popular publishes the impairment for credit risk as a total of 8,237 Mio. € for 2014 and 8,366 Mio. € for 2013 (Annual report 2014, p. 346), so it decreased by 129 Mio. €. While the loans impairments were 1,691 Mio. € in 2014 (Annual report 2014, p. 167), the default must have been 1,691 Mio. € + 129 Mio. € = 1,820 Mio. €.

Position	Amount (€m)
Interest income	4,181
Interest expense	1,836
Cost of risk	−1,691
Net interest income after cost of risk	654
Commission income	739
Commission expense	85
Net commission income	654
Trading income	821
Salaries	946
Other operating expenses	941
Depreciation, amortisation and impairments	145
Income before tax	373
Income tax	43
Income after tax	330
Income from discontinued operations after tax	0
Net income	330
Extraordinary income	124

Banco Popular is lightly profitable. Again the high cost of risk is the main problem.

An expected allocation ratio of 0.5% would lead to a cost of risk of 107,828 Mio. € (Loans to customers, Annual report 2014, p. 210) × 0.5% = 539 Mio. €. With this amount, Banco Popular would reach a net income of +1,482 Mio. €.

With risk-weighted assets of 80,113 Mio. € (Annual report 2014, p. 78), it has a RoRWA of 330 / 80,113 = 0.41%. The bank is profitable but not strongly profitable.

6.8 Banco Santander

Banco Santander published the following data from its profit and loss account (Annual report 2014, p. 386):

Position	Amount (€m)
Interest income	54,656
Interest expense	25,109
Cost of risk	−10,521
Net interest income after cost of risk	19,026
Commission income	12,515
Commission expense	2,819
Net commission income	9,696
Trading income	2,377
Net insurance income	137
Net income from other activities	−361
Salaries	10,242
Other operating expenses	7,657
Depreciation, amortisation and impairments	2,287
Income before tax	10,679
Income tax	3,718
Income after tax	6,961
Income from discontinued operations after tax	−26
Net income	6,935

We have to make the following reclassifications:

- In net income from other activities there is the dividend income of +435 Mio. €. This has to be reclassified to interest income.

- In net income from other activities there are net provisions of −3,009 Mio. €. This has to be reclassified to operating expenses.

- All other amounts in the net income from other activities are extraordinary.

Position	Amount (€m)
Interest income	55,091
Interest expense	25,109
Cost of risk	−10,521
Net interest income after cost of risk	19,461
Commission income	12,515
Commission expense	2,819
Net commission income	9,696
Trading income	2,377
Net insurance income	137
Salaries	10,242
Other operating expenses	10,666
Depreciation, amortisation and impairments	2,287
Income before tax	8,466
Income tax	3,718
Income after tax	4,748
Income from discontinued operations after tax	−26
Net income	4,722
Extraordinary income	2,213

Banco Santander is profitable but not strongly profitable. With risk-weighted assets of 585,243 Mio. € (Annual report 2014, p. 118), it has a RoRWA of 4,722 / 585,243 = 0.81%. The reason for this low RoRWA is the high allocation ratio of 10,521 / 774,125 = 1.36%. A positive is the low influence of trading income on net income.

6.9 Bank of Ireland

Bank of Ireland published the following data from its profit and loss account (Annual report 2014, p. 156):

Position	Amount (€m)
Interest income	3,432
Interest expense	1,111
Cost of risk	542
Net interest income after cost of risk	1,779
Commission income	558
Commission expense	214
Net commission income	344
Trading income	−42
Insurance income	2,158
Insurance expenses	2,079
Net income from other activities	465
Salaries	855
Other operating expenses	741
Depreciation, amortisation and impairments	109
Income before tax	920
Income tax	134
Income after tax	786
Income from discontinued operations after tax	0
Net income	786

We have to make the following reclassifications:

- In net income from other activities there is dividend income of +11 Mio. €. This has to be reclassified to interest income.

- All other amounts in the net income from other activities are extraordinary because they come from non-banking activities like rental income.

- Bank of Ireland publishes defaults of 1,630 Mio. € (Annual report 2014, p. 218).

Position	Amount (€m)
Interest income	3,443
Interest expense	1,111
Cost of risk	542
Net interest income after cost of risk	1,790
Commission income	558
Commission expense	214
Net commission income	344
Trading income	−42
Insurance income	2,158
Insurance expenses	2,079
Salaries	855
Other operating expenses	741
Depreciation, amortisation and impairments	109
Income before tax	464
Income tax	134
Income after tax	330
Income from discontinued operations after tax	0
Net income	330
Extraordinary income	454

Bank of Ireland is highly profitable. This is mostly dependent on the cost of risk, which was down significantly in 2014. While in 2013 the cost of risk was 1,665 Mio. €, it decreased to 542 Mio. € in 2014. This is the only reason why 2014 was profitable. With the same cost of risk as 2013, Bank of Ireland would still be unprofitable.

The default ratio in 2014 is 1,630 / 82,118 = 1.98% with an allocation ratio of 542 / 82,118 = 0.66%. Bank of Ireland will only stay profitable if the default ratio goes down to the same level as the allocation ratio. If the default ratio stays constant, the allocation ratio has to increase again, which makes the bank unprofitable.

With risk-weighted assets of 51,600 Mio. € (Annual report 2014, p. 14), it has a RoRWA of 330 / 51,600 = 0.64%. The bank is profitable but not strongly profitable.

6.10 Bankia

Bankia published the following data from its profit and loss account (Annual report 2014, p. 2):

Position	Amount (€m)
Interest income	4,687
Interest expense	1,760
Cost of risk	−973
Net interest income after cost of risk	1,954
Commission income	1,036
Commission expense	88
Net commission income	948
Trading income	−49
Net insurance income	-3
Net income from other activities	−194

Position	Amount (€m)
Salaries	987
Other operating expenses	599
Depreciation, amortisation and impairments	156
Income before tax	912
Income tax	226
Income after tax	686
Income from discontinued operations after tax	85
Net income	771

We have to make the following reclassifications:

- In net income from other activities there is dividend income of +5 Mio. €. This has to be reclassified to interest income.

- In net income from other activities there are net provisions of −208 Mio. €. This has to be reclassified to operating expenses.

- All other amounts in the net income from other activities are extraordinary.

Position	Amount (€m)
Interest income	4,692
Interest expense	1,760
Cost of risk	−973
Net interest income after cost of risk	1,959
Commission income	1,036
Commission expense	88
Net commission income	948
Trading income	−49
Net insurance income	−3

Position	Amount (€m)
Salaries	987
Other operating expenses	807
Depreciation, amortisation and impairments	156
Income before tax	903
Income tax	226
Income after tax	677
Income from discontinued operations after tax	85
Net income	762
Extraordinary income	9

Bankia is profitable. With risk-weighted assets of 88,565 Mio. € (Annual report 2014, p. 21), it has a RoRWA of 677 / 88,565 = 0.76%. The bank is profitable but not strongly profitable. Bankia mostly depends on the cost of risk. The allocation ratio in 2014 is 973 / 123,659 = 0.79% after 1,236 / 128,335 = 0.96% in 2013.

6.11 Bankinter

Bankinter published the following data from its profit and loss account (Annual report 2014, p. 6):

Position	Amount (€m)
Interest income	1,404
Interest expense	649
Cost of risk	−234
Net interest income after cost of risk	521
Commission income	365

Position	Amount (€m)
Commission expense	74
Net commission income	291
Trading income	15
Net insurance income	289
Net income from other activities	−14
Salaries	369
Other operating expenses	287
Depreciation, amortisation and impairments	64
Income before tax	393
Income tax	117
Income after tax	276
Income from discontinued operations after tax	0
Net income	276

We have to make the following reclassifications:

- In net income from other activities there is dividend income of +8 Mio. €. This has to be reclassified to interest income.

- In net income from other activities there are net provisions of −42 Mio. €. This has to be reclassified to operating expenses.

- All other amounts in the net income from other activities are extraordinary.

Position	Amount (€m)
Interest income	1,412
Interest expense	649
Cost of risk	−234
Net interest income after cost of risk	529

Position	Amount (€m)
Commission income	365
Commission expense	74
Net commission income	291
Trading income	15
Net insurance income	289
Salaries	369
Other operating expenses	329
Depreciation, amortisation and impairments	64
Income before tax	373
Income tax	117
Income after tax	256
Income from discontinued operations after tax	0
Net income	256
Extraordinary income	20

Bankinter is profitable. With risk-weighted assets of 25,704 Mio. €
(Annual report 2014, p. 22), it has a RoRWA of 256 / 25,704 = 1.00%.
Especially good for profitability is the cost of risk getting lower and
lower. The allocation ratio in 2014 is 234 / 43,560 = 0.54% after 281 /
42,489 = 0.66% in 2013.

6.12 Barclays

Barclays published the following data from its profit and loss account (Annual report 2014, p. 255):

Position	Amount (GBP m)
Interest income	17,363
Interest expense	5,283
Cost of risk	−2,168
Net interest income after cost of risk	9,912
Commission income	9,836
Commission expense	1,662
Net commission income	8,174
Trading income	3,331
Insurance income	669
Insurance expenses	480
Net income from other activities	1,079
Salaries	11,005
Other operating expenses	8,145
Depreciation, amortisation and impairments	1,279
Income before tax	2,256
Income tax	1,411
Income after tax	845
Income from discontinued operations after tax	0
Net income	845

We have to make the following reclassifications:

- In net income from other activities there is dividend income of +9 Mio. GBP. This has to be reclassified to interest income.

- In net income from other activities there is a net gain from disposal of available-for-sale investments of +620 Mio. GBP. This has to be reclassified to extraordinary income.

- In other operating expenses an amount of 1,250 Mio. GBP is included for provision for ongoing investigations and litigation relating to foreign exchange. This is hopefully a one-time expense, so we have to deal with it with a special kind of analysis.

- All other amounts in the net income from other activities are extraordinary because they come from non-banking activities like rental income.

- Barclays publishes the impairment for credit risk as a total of 5,455 Mio. GBP for 2014 and 7,258 Mio. GBP for 2013 (Annual report 2014, p. 297), so it decreased by 1,703 Mio. GBP. While the loans impairments were 2,168 Mio. GBP in 2014 (Annual report 2014, p. 255), the default must have been 2,168 Mio. GBP + 1,703 Mio. GBP = 3,871 Mio. GBP.

Position	Amount (GBP m)
Interest income	17,372
Interest expense	5,283
Cost of risk	−2,168
Net interest income after cost of risk	9,921
Commission income	9,836
Commission expense	1,662
Net commission income	8,174
Trading income	3,331
Insurance income	669
Insurance expenses	480

Position	Amount (GBP m)
Salaries	11,005
Other operating expenses	8,145
Depreciation, amortisation and impairments	1,279
Income before tax	1,186
Income tax	1,411
Income after tax	−225
Income from discontinued operations after tax	0
Net income	−225
Extraordinary income	1,070

Barclays is lightly unprofitable, mostly because of the provision for ongoing investigations and litigations mentioned above. Without this, Barclays would be profitable.

Additionally, the cost of risk has to be mentioned. The default ratio in 2014 is 3,871 / 469,878 = 0.82% with an allocation ratio of 2,168 / 469,878 = 0.46%. Only if the default ratio goes down to the level of the allocation ratio can Barclays be profitable. If not, further provisions for litigation will be needed. If the default ratio stays constant, the allocation ratio has to increase again, which makes the bank unprofitable.

With risk-weighted assets of 402,000 Mio. GBP (Annual report 2014, p. 186) and excluding the provisions for further investigations and litigation, it has a RoRWA of 1,025 / 402,000 = 0.25%. The bank is only very lightly profitable. The RoRWA is much too low.

6.13 Banca Popolare di Sondrio

Banca Popolare di Sondrio published the following data from its profit and loss account (Annual report 2014, p. 142):

Position	Amount (€m)
Interest income	860
Interest expense	339
Cost of risk	–454
Net interest income after cost of risk	67
Commission income	258
Commission expense	16
Net commission income	242
Trading income	90
Net income from other activities	169
Salaries	176
Other operating expenses	206
Depreciation, amortisation and impairments	25
Income before tax	162
Income tax	64
Income after tax	98
Income from discontinued operations after tax	0
Net income	98

We have to make the following reclassifications:

- In net income from other activities there is dividend income of +16 Mio. €. This has to be reclassified to interest income.

- In net income from other activities there are gains/losses from sales or repurchases of +94 Mio. €. This has to be reclassified to extraordinary income.
- All other amounts in the net income from other activities are extraordinary.

Position	Amount (€m)
Interest income	876
Interest expense	339
Cost of risk	−454
Net interest income after cost of risk	83
Commission income	258
Commission expense	16
Net commission income	242
Trading income	90
Salaries	176
Other operating expenses	206
Depreciation, amortisation and impairments	25
Income before tax	9
Income tax	64
Income after tax	−55
Income from discontinued operations after tax	0
Net income	−55
Extraordinary income	153

Banca Popolare di Sondrio is lightly unprofitable, mostly because of the very high cost of risk with an allocation ratio of 454 / 25,100 = 1.81%. Unfortunately, this bank does not give enough information in the notes to further analyse the cost of risk, but we can say that this amount is much too high for operating income. The cost of risk will have to fall strongly in the near future, but it is not possible to calculate what amount to expect.

With risk-weighted assets of 21,338 Mio. € (Annual report 2014, p. 287), it has a RoRWA of -55 / 21,338 = -0.26%. For an Italian bank in 2014 this is relatively good, but still unprofitable. With an allocation ratio of 0.5% = 126 Mio. €, Banca Popolare di Sondrio would reach a net income of 273 Mio. € and a RoRWA of 1.28%. In contrast to other Italian banks, all this bank needs to do to reach good performance is reduce the cost of risk.

6.14 Banca Popolare dell'Emilia Romagna

Banca Popolare dell'Emilia Romagna published the following data from its profit and loss account (Annual report 2014, p. 136):

Position	Amount (€m)
Interest income	1,908
Interest expense	616
Cost of risk	−813
Net interest income after cost of risk	478
Commission income	739
Commission expense	48
Net commission income	691
Trading income	17
Net income from other activities	258
Salaries	787
Other operating expenses	530

Position	Amount (€m)
Depreciation, amortisation and impairments	70
Income before tax	58
Income tax	28
Income after tax	30
Income from discontinued operations after tax	0
Net income	30

We have to make the following reclassifications:

- In net income from other activities there is dividend income of +19 Mio. €. This has to be reclassified to interest income.

- In net income from other activities there are gains/losses on disposal or repurchases of +164 Mio. €. This has to be reclassified to extraordinary income.

- In net income from other activities there is a net provision for risks and charges of 39 Mio. €. This has to be reclassified to operating expenses.

- All other amounts in the net income from other activities are extraordinary.

Position	Amount (€m)
Interest income	1,927
Interest expense	616
Cost of risk	–813
Net interest income after cost of risk	497
Commission income	739
Commission expense	48
Net commission income	691
Trading income	17

Position	Amount (€m)
Salaries	787
Other operating expenses	569
Depreciation, amortisation and impairments	70
Income before tax	−220
Income tax	28
Income after tax	−248
Income from discontinued operations after tax	0
Net income	−248
Extraordinary income	278

Banca Popolare dell'Emilia Romagna is lightly unprofitable, mostly because of the very high cost of risk with an allocation ratio of 813 / 45,629 = 1.78%. Unfortunately, this bank also does not give enough information in the notes to further analyse the cost of risk, but we can say that this amount is much too high for operating income. The cost of risk will have to fall strongly in the near future, but it is not possible to calculate what amount to expect.

With risk-weighted assets of 40,692 Mio. € (Annual report 2014, p. 389), it has a RoRWA of −248 / 40,692 = −0.61%. For an Italian bank in 2014, this is an acceptable value, but still unprofitable. With an allocation ratio of 0.5% = 228 Mio. €, Banca Popolare dell'Emilia Romagna would reach a net income of 237 Mio. € and a RoRWA of 0.58%. In contrast to other Italian banks, all this bank needs to do to reach good performance is reduce the cost of risk.

6.15 BNP Paribas

BNP Paribas published the following data from its profit and loss account (Annual report 2014, p. 4):

Position	Amount (€m)
Interest income	38,707
Interest expense	18,388
Cost of risk	–3,705
Net interest income after cost of risk	16,614
Commission income	12,661
Commission expense	5,273
Net commission income	7,388
Trading income	4,631
Net income from other activities	1,042
Salaries	14,801
Other operating expenses	10,159
Depreciation, amortisation and impairments	1,566
Income before tax	3,149
Income tax	2,642
Income after tax	507
Income from discontinued operations after tax	0
Net income	507

We have to make the following reclassifications:

- In net income from other activities there is dividend income of 534 Mio. €. This has to be reclassified to interest income.

- In net income from other activities there is net insurance income of +3,441 Mio. €. This has to be reclassified to operating income.

- In net income from other activities there is leasing income of +1,085 Mio. €. This has to be reclassified to interest income.

- In net income from other activities there are costs related to the comprehensive settlement with US authorities of −6,000 Mio. €. We will treat this as extraordinary, but it has to be investigated further.

- All other amounts in the net income from other activities are extraordinary.

Position	Amount (€m)
Interest income	40,326
Interest expense	18,388
Cost of risk	−3,705
Net interest income after cost of risk	18,233
Commission income	12,661
Commission expense	5,273
Net commission income	7,388
Trading income	4,631
Net insurance income	3,441
Salaries	14,801
Other operating expenses	10,159
Depreciation, amortisation and impairments	1,566
Income before tax	7,167
Income tax	2,642
Income after tax	4,525
Income from discontinued operations after tax	0
Net income	4,525
Extraordinary income	−4,018

BNP Paribas is profitable. With risk-weighted assets of 619,827 Mio. € (Annual report 2014, p. 264), it has a RoRWA of 4,525 / 619,827 = 0.73%. The RoRWA of BNP Paribas is much too low, especially because we treat the costs related to the comprehensive settlement with US authorities as extraordinary, without knowing the risk situation of BNP Paribas in this direction.

6.16 Caixabank

Caixabank published the following data from its profit and loss account (Annual report 2014, p. 3):

Position	Amount (€m)
Interest income	8,791
Interest expense	4,637
Cost of risk	−2,054
Net interest income after cost of risk	2,100
Commission income	1,973
Commission expense	148
Net commission income	1,825
Trading income	−42
Net insurance income	149
Net income from other activities	−559
Salaries	2,578
Other operating expenses	846
Depreciation, amortisation and impairments	350
Income before tax	202
Income tax	−418
Income after tax	620

Position	Amount (€m)
Income from discontinued operations after tax	0
Net income	620

We have to make the following reclassifications:

- In net income from other activities there is dividend income of 185 Mio. €. This has to be reclassified to interest income.

- In net income from other activities there is a contribution to the deposit guarantee fund of −293 Mio. €. This has to be reclassified to operating expenses.

- All other amounts in the net income from other activities are extraordinary.

Position	Amount (€m)
Interest income	8,976
Interest expense	4,637
Cost of risk	−2,054
Net interest income after cost of risk	2,285
Commission income	1,973
Commission expense	148
Net commission income	1,825
Trading income	−42
Net insurance income	149
Salaries	2,578
Other operating expenses	1,139
Depreciation, amortisation and impairments	350
Income before tax	653
Income tax	−418

Position	Amount (€m)
Income after tax	1,071
Income from discontinued operations after tax	0
Net income	1,071
Extraordinary income	–451

Caixabank is lightly profitable. Because Caixabank got a tax refund while having a profit, we have to calculate a *normal* income after tax: 70% × 653 Mio. € = 457 Mio. €. With risk-weighted assets of 139,729 Mio. € (Annual report 2014, p. 35), it has a RoRWA of 457 / 139,729 = 0.33%. The RoRWA of Caixabank is very low, especially because of the cost of risk. The allocation ratio in 2014 is 2,054 / 193,139 = 1.06%, down from 3,974 / 203,970 = 1.95% in 2013.

6.17 Commerzbank

Commerzbank published the following data from its profit and loss account (Annual report 2014, p. 136):

Position	Amount (€m)
Interest income	12,555
Interest expense	6,948
Cost of risk	–1,144
Net interest income after cost of risk	4,463
Commission income	3,837
Commission expense	632
Net commission income	3,205
Trading income	377

Position	Amount (€m)
Net income from other activities	-374
Salaries	3,843
Other operating expenses	2,637
Depreciation, amortisation and impairments	446
Income before tax	623
Income tax	253
Income after tax	370
Income from discontinued operations after tax	0
Net income	370

We have to make the following reclassifications:

- In net income from other activities there is a provision of −949 Mio. €. This has to be reclassified to operating expenses.

- All other amounts in the net income from other activities are extraordinary.

Position	Amount (€m)
Interest income	12,555
Interest expense	6,948
Cost of risk	−1,144
Net interest income after cost of risk	4,463
Commission income	3,837
Commission expense	632
Net commission income	3,205
Trading income	377
Salaries	3,843

Position	Amount (€m)
Other operating expenses	3,586
Depreciation, amortisation and impairments	446
Income before tax	48
Income tax	253
Income after tax	−205
Income from discontinued operations after tax	0
Net income	−205
Extraordinary income	575

Commerzbank is lightly unprofitable. With risk-weighted assets of 215,178 Mio. € (Annual report 2014, p. 270), it has a RoRWA of −205 / 215,278 = −0.10%. The allocation ratio is 1,144 / 312,903 = 0.37%, so from this side no positive effects can be expected in the long run.

Compared to the net commission income, the net interest income after the cost of risk is too low. With the actual cost basis, it will be hard for Commerzbank to become a really profitable bank.

6.18 Credit Suisse

Credit Suisse published the following data from its profit and loss account (Annual report 2014, p. 259):

Position	Amount (CHF m)
Interest income	19,061
Interest expense	10,027
Cost of risk	−186
Net interest income after cost of risk	8,848

Position	Amount (CHF m)
Commission income	13,051
Commission expense	1,561
Net commission income	11,490
Trading income	2,026
Net income from other activities	2,131
Salaries	11,334
Other operating expenses	8,255
Depreciation, amortisation and impairments	1,279
Income before tax	3,627
Income tax	1,405
Income after tax	2,324
Income from discontinued operations after tax	0
Net income	2,324

We have to make the following reclassifications:

- Credit Suisse puts the interest income and interest expenses for trading securities in the interest income and expenses. For analysis we have to reclassify +9,503 Mio. CHF and −3,938 Mio. CHF to trading income.

- All amounts in the net income from other activities are extraordinary.

Position	Amount (CHF m)
Interest income	9,558
Interest expense	6,089
Cost of risk	−186
Net interest income after cost of risk	3,283

Position	Amount (CHF m)
Commission income	13,051
Commission expense	1,561
Net commission income	11,490
Trading income	7,591
Salaries	11,334
Other operating expenses	8,255
Depreciation, amortisation and impairments	1,279
Income before tax	1,496
Income tax	1,405
Income after tax	91
Income from discontinued operations after tax	102
Net income	193
Extraordinary income	2,131

Credit Suisse is lightly profitable. With risk-weighted assets of 291,410 Mio. CHF (Annual report 2014, p. 388), it has a RoRWA of 91 / 291,410 = 0.03%. In contrast to other banks, the cost of risk is unimportant. Credit Suisse is mostly an investment bank, so it is largely dependent on net commission income and trading income, while net interest income ranks only third in earnings.

Because of the high risk in trading income and also in net commission income, the profitability of Credit Suisse is much too low.

6.19 Crédit Agricole

Crédit Agricole published the following data from its profit and loss account (Annual report 2014, p. 151):

Position	Amount (€m)
Interest income	37,037
Interest expense	17,521
Cost of risk	−2,943
Net interest income after cost of risk	16,573
Commission income	11,500
Commission expense	2,683
Net commission income	8,817
Trading income	5,942
Insurance income	−7,275
Net income from other activities	2,884
Salaries	11,044
Other operating expenses	7,117
Depreciation, amortisation and impairments	1,017
Income before tax	7,763
Income tax	2,477
Income after tax	5,286
Income from discontinued operations after tax	−7
Net income	5,279

We have to make the following reclassifications:

- In net income from other activities there is dividend income of 902 Mio. €. This has to be reclassified to interest income.

- All other amounts in the net income from other activities are extraordinary.

Position	Amount (€m)
Interest income	37,939
Interest expense	17,521
Cost of risk	−2,943
Net interest income after cost of risk	17,475
Commission income	11,500
Commission expense	2,683
Net commission income	8,817
Trading income	5,942
Insurance income	−7,275
Salaries	11,044
Other operating expenses	7,117
Depreciation, amortisation and impairments	1,017
Income before tax	5,781
Income tax	2,477
Income after tax	3,304
Income from discontinued operations after tax	−7
Net income	3,297
Extraordinary income	1,982

Crédit Agricole is strongly profitable. With risk-weighted assets of 494,934 Mio. € (Annual report 2014, p. 91), it has a RoRWA of 3,297 / 494,934 = 0.67%. The RoRWA is quite low.

On first view, the net interest income after cost of risk looks very high. Here we have to note that Crédit Agricole has a big insurance business and the provisions for the customers are in another income position while the earnings are mostly in interest income. If we subtract insurance income from net interest income after cost of risk, around 10 billion € is for the bank only. Compared to the net commission income, this is a bit too low.

As well as trading income being very high for a retail bank, Crédit Agricole has higher risks than a normal retail bank in its income statement. For these risks, the RoRWA is much too low.

6.20 Danske Bank

Danske Bank published the following data from its profit and loss account (Annual report 2014, p. 46):

Position	Amount (DKK m)
Interest income	66,951
Interest expense	32,344
Cost of risk	–3,718
Net interest income after cost of risk	30,889
Commission income	14,585
Commission expense	4,771
Net commission income	9,814
Trading income	9,720
Net income from other activities	–4,552
Insurance income	–12,393
Salaries	14,121
Other operating expenses	8,909
Depreciation, amortisation and impairments	2,612
Income before tax	7,835
Income tax	3,989

Position	Amount (DKK m)
Income after tax	3,846
Income from discontinued operations after tax	0
Net income	3,846

We have to make the following reclassifications:

- In net income from other activities there is leasing income of 2,540 Mio. DKK. This has to be reclassified to interest income.

- All other amounts in the net income from other activities are extraordinary.

- Danske Bank publishes the impairment for credit risk at a total of 35,732 Mio. DKK for 2014 and 41,739 Mio. DKK for 2013 (Annual report 2014, p. 81), so it decreased by 6,007 Mio. DKK. While the loans impairments were 3,718 Mio. DKK in 2014 (Annual report 2014, p. 46), the default must have been 3,718 Mio. € + 6,007 Mio. € = 9,725 Mio. €.

Position	Amount (DKK m)
Interest income	69,491
Interest expense	32,344
Cost of risk	–3,718
Net interest income after cost of risk	33,429
Commission income	14,585
Commission expense	4,771
Net commission income	9,814
Trading income	9,720
Insurance income	–12,393
Salaries	14,121
Other operating expenses	8,909

Position	Amount (DKK m)
Depreciation, amortisation and impairments	2,612
Income before tax	14,927
Income tax	3,989
Income after tax	10,938
Income from discontinued operations after tax	0
Net income	10,938
Extraordinary income	−7,092

Danske Bank is strongly profitable. With risk-weighted assets of 866,000 Mio. DKK (Annual report 2014, p. 37), it has a RoRWA of 10,938 / 866,000 = 1.26%. The RoRWA is quite high.

On first view, the net interest income after cost of risk looks very high. Here we have to note that Danske Bank has a big insurance business and the provisions for the customers are in another income position while the earnings are mostly in interest income. If we subtract insurance income from net interest income after cost of risk, around 20 billion DKK is for the bank only. Compared to the net commission income, this is still very high.

Unfortunately, trading income is very high, so Danske Bank has higher risks than a normal retail bank in its income statement. For these risks, the RoRWA is reasonable, but not especially high.

6.21 Deutsche Bank

Deutsche Bank published the following data from its profit and loss account (Annual report 2014, p. 349):

Position	Amount (€m)
Interest income	25,001
Interest expense	10,729
Cost of risk	−1,134
Net interest income after cost of risk	13,138
Commission income	15,746
Commission expense	3,337
Net commission income	12,409
Trading income	4,299
Net income from other activities	436
Salaries	12,512
Other operating expenses	13,992
Depreciation, amortisation and impairments	662
Income before tax	3,116
Income tax	1,425
Income after tax	1,691
Income from discontinued operations after tax	0
Net income	1,691

We have to make the following reclassifications:

- In net income from other activities there is net income from hedge relationships qualifying for hedge accounting of −1,349 Mio. €. This has to be reclassified to interest expenses.

- All other amounts in the net income from other activities are extraordinary.

Position	Amount (€m)
Interest income	25,001
Interest expense	12,078
Cost of risk	−1,134
Net interest income after cost of risk	11,789
Commission income	15,746
Commission expense	3,337
Net commission income	12,409
Trading income	4,299
Net income from other activities	436
Salaries	12,512
Other operating expenses	13,992
Depreciation, amortisation and impairments	662
Income before tax	1,331
Income tax	1,425
Income after tax	−94
Income from discontinued operations after tax	0
Net income	−94
Extraordinary income	1,785

Deutsche Bank is lightly unprofitable. With risk-weighted assets of 393,969 Mio. € (Annual report 2014, p. 263), it has a RoRWA of −94 / 393,969 = −0.02%. The RoRWA is very low.

Deutsche Bank is an investment bank, so the risk is much higher than for a retail bank. For an investment bank, the RoRWA is much too low. Additionally, in section 3.2 I discussed the provisions of Deutsche Bank. It is important to remember the high risks in this specific area.

6.22 DNB

DNB published the following data from its profit and loss account (Annual report 2014, p. 110):

Position	Amount (NOK m)
Interest income	61,445
Interest expense	28,959
Cost of risk	−1,639
Net interest income after cost of risk	30,848
Commission income	11,565
Commission expense	2,597
Net commission income	8,968
Trading income	5,317
Insurance result	1,100
Net income from other activities	1,542
Salaries	10,872
Other operating expenses	7,645
Depreciation, amortisation and impairments	2,158
Income before tax	27,102
Income tax	6,463
Income after tax	20,639
Income from discontinued operations after tax	−22
Net income	20,617

We have to make the following reclassifications:

- All amounts in the net income from other activities are extraordinary.

Position	Amount (NOK m)
Interest income	61,445
Interest expense	28,959
Cost of risk	−1,639
Net interest income after cost of risk	30,848
Commission income	11,565
Commission expense	2,597
Net commission income	8,968
Trading income	5,317
Insurance result	1,100
Salaries	10,872
Other operating expenses	7,645
Depreciation, amortisation and impairments	2,158
Income before tax	25,560
Income tax	6,463
Income after tax	19,097
Income from discontinued operations after tax	−22
Net income	19,075
Extraordinary income	1,542

DNB is strongly profitable. It has risk-weighted assets of 1,120,659 Mio. NOK (Annual report 2014, p. 131), it has a RoRWA of 19,075 / 1,120,659 = 1.70%. The RoRWA is very high. It has to be said that DNB's main income source is the net interest income after cost of risk. Both net commission income and trading income are of lower importance. Even with only the net interest income after cost of risk, DNB would already be profitable.

6.23 Erste Group Bank

Erste Group Bank published the following data from its profit and loss account (Annual report 2014, p. 349):

Position	Amount (€m)
Interest income	6,984
Interest expense	4,685
Cost of risk	−1,774
Net interest income after cost of risk	2,911
Commission income	2,306
Commission expense	499
Net commission income	1,806
Trading income	219
Net income from other activities	−983
Salaries	2,232
Other operating expenses	1,146
Depreciation, amortisation and impairments	518
Income before tax	378
Income tax	179
Income after tax	200
Income from discontinued operations after tax	0
Net income	200

We have to make the following reclassifications:

- In interest income Erste Group Bank has included interest income from financial assets held for trading of +522 Mio. € and interest expenses of −160 Mio. €. This has to be reclassified to trading income.

- In net income from other activities there is dividend income of 90 Mio. €. This has to be reclassified to interest income.

- In net income from other activities there are taxes for bank business of −311 Mio. €. This has to be reclassified to operating expenses.

- In net income from other activities there is a provision of −77 Mio. €. This has to be reclassified to operating expenses.

- All other amounts in the net income from other activities are extraordinary.

Position	Amount (€m)
Interest income	6,552
Interest expense	2,139
Cost of risk	−1,774
Net interest income after cost of risk	2,639
Commission income	2,306
Commission expense	499
Net commission income	1,806
Trading income	581
Salaries	2,232
Other operating expenses	1,534
Depreciation, amortisation and impairments	518
Income before tax	−307
Income tax	179
Income after tax	−485
Income from discontinued operations after tax	0
Net income	−485
Extraordinary income	−685

Erste Group Bank is unprofitable. With risk-weighted assets of 100,885 Mio. € (Annual report 2014, p. 252), it has a RoRWA of −485 / 100,885 = −0.48%. The RoRWA is very low.

Erste Group Bank's biggest problems come from daughter companies in Eastern Europe. Its allocation ratio is 1,774 / 128,276 = 1.38%. With an allocation ratio of 0.5%, Erste Group Bank would make a net income of 648 Mio. € and a RoRWA of 0.64%. Even this would be too low.

Erste Group Bank seems to have a particular problem on the cost side.

6.24 HSBC

HSBC published the following data from its profit and loss account (Annual report 2014, p. 349):

Position	Amount (US-$ m)
Interest income	50,955
Interest expense	16,250
Cost of risk	−3,851
Net interest income after cost of risk	30,854
Commission income	19,545
Commission expense	3,588
Net commission income	15,957
Trading income	6,760
Net income from other activities	10,253
Net insurance income	−1,424
Salaries	20,366
Other operating expenses	18,565
Depreciation, amortisation and impairments	2,218
Income before tax	18,680

Position	Amount (US-$ m)
Income tax	3,975
Income after tax	14,705
Income from discontinued operations after tax	0
Net income	14,705

We have to make the following reclassifications:

- In net income from other activities there is dividend income of 311 Mio. US-$. This has to be reclassified to interest income.

- In net income from other activities there is a share of profit in associates and joint ventures of 2,532 Mio. US-$. This has to be reclassified to operating income, because it is coming from joint ventures with other banks.

- In net income from other activities there is net income from financial instruments designated at fair value of 2,473 Mio. US-$. This income comes from the insurance business, so it has to be reclassified to the insurance income.

- All other amounts in the net income from other activities are extraordinary.

Position	Amount (US-$ m)
Interest income	51,266
Interest expense	16,250
Cost of risk	−3,851
Net interest income after cost of risk	31,165
Commission income	19,545
Commission expense	3,588
Net commission income	15,957
Trading income	6,760

Position	Amount (US-$ m)
Operating income (share of profits in associates)	2,532
Net insurance income	1,049
Salaries	20,366
Other operating expenses	18,565
Depreciation, amortisation and impairments	2,218
Income before tax	13,743
Income tax	3,975
Income after tax	9,768
Income from discontinued operations after tax	0
Net income	9,768
Extraordinary income	4,937

HSBC is strongly profitable from its net income. With risk-weighted assets of 1,219,765 Mio. US-$ (Annual report 2014, p. 239), it has a RoRWA of 9,768 / 1,219,765 = 0.80%. The RoRWA is quite low. It is positive that HSBC's income comes mostly from net interest income after cost of risk, while the trading income is quite low compared to interest and commission income.

6.25 Intesa Sanpaolo

Intesa Sanpaolo published the following data from its profit and loss account (Annual report 2014, p. 166):

Position	Amount (€m)
Interest income	15,933
Interest expense	6,116
Cost of risk	–4,102
Net interest income after cost of risk	5,715
Commission income	8,058
Commission expense	1,591
Net commission income	6,467
Trading income	210
Net income from other activities	1,197
Net insurance income	–2,205
Salaries	5,268
Other operating expenses	3,574
Depreciation, amortisation and impairments	973
Income before tax	3,009
Income tax	1,651
Income after tax	1,358
Income from discontinued operations after tax	–48
Net income	1,310

We have to make the following reclassifications:

- In net income from other activities there is dividend income of 315 Mio. €. This has to be reclassified to interest income.

- In net income from other activities there are fair value adjustments in hedge accounting of −139 Mio. €. This has to be reclassified to interest expenses.

- In net income from other activities there are net provisions for risk and charges of 546 Mio. €. This has to be reclassified to operating expenses.

- All other amounts in the net income from other activities are extraordinary.

Position	Amount (€m)
Interest income	16,248
Interest expense	6,255
Cost of risk	−4,102
Net interest income after cost of risk	5,891
Commission income	8,058
Commission expense	1,591
Net commission income	6,467
Trading income	210
Net insurance income	−2,205
Salaries	5,268
Other operating expenses	4,120
Depreciation, amortisation and impairments	973
Income before tax	1,442
Income tax	1,651
Income after tax	−209
Income from discontinued operations after tax	-48
Net income	−257
Extraordinary income	1,567

Intesa Sanpaolo is lightly unprofitable. With risk-weighted assets of 269,790 Mio. € (Annual report 2014, p. 423), it has a RoRWA of −257 / 269,790 = −0.10%. The negative income is mostly dependent on the allocation ratio of 4,102 / 370,477 = 1.11%. For an Italian bank in 2014 this is very good, but the bank is still unprofitable.

With an allocation ratio of 0.5% = 1,852 Mio. €, Intesa Sanpaolo would reach a net income of 1,993 Mio. € and a RoRWA of 0.74%. In contrast to other Italian banks, this bank can reach a good performance only with a lower cost of risk.

6.26 Julius Bär

Julius Bär published the following data from its profit and loss account (Annual report 2014, p. 46):

Position	Amount (CHF m)
Interest income	780
Interest expense	132
Cost of risk	0
Net interest income after cost of risk	648
Commission income	1,726
Commission expense	208
Net commission income	1,518
Trading income	328
Net income from other activities	53
Salaries	1,259
Other operating expenses	609
Depreciation, amortisation and impairments	209
Income before tax	470

Position	Amount (CHF m)
Income tax	103
Income after tax	367
Income from discontinued operations after tax	0
Net income	367

We have to make the following reclassifications:

- In interest income Julius Bär has included interest income from financial assets held for trading of +162 Mio. €. This has to be reclassified to trading income.

- All amounts in the net income from other activities are extraordinary.

Position	Amount (CHF m)
Interest income	618
Interest expense	132
Cost of risk	0
Net interest income after cost of risk	486
Commission income	1,726
Commission expense	208
Net commission income	1,518
Trading income	490
Salaries	1,259
Other operating expenses	609
Depreciation, amortisation and impairments	209
Income before tax	417
Income tax	103
Income after tax	314

Position	Amount (CHF m)
Income from discontinued operations after tax	0
Net income	314
Extraordinary income	53

Julius Bär is highly profitable. With risk-weighted assets of 16,978 Mio. CHF (Annual report 2014, p. 87), it has a RoRWA of 314 / 16,978 = 1.85%. But it has to be mentioned that Julius Bär is not really comparable to the other banks used in this book, because it is only active in private banking. We cannot use it as a benchmark for this reason.

6.27 Jyske Bank

Jyske Bank published the following data from its profit and loss account (Annual report 2014, p. 43):

Position	Amount (DKK m)
Interest income	11,268
Interest expense	4,653
Cost of risk	−2,538
Net interest income after cost of risk	4,077
Commission income	2,102
Commission expense	343
Net commission income	1,759
Trading income	0
Net income from other activities	2,800
Salaries	3,020

Position	Amount (DKK m)
Other operating expenses	2,089
Depreciation, amortisation and impairments	424
Income before tax	3,103
Income tax	14
Income after tax	3,089
Income from discontinued operations after tax	0
Net income	3,089

We have to make the following reclassifications:

- In net income from other activities there are value adjustments of −653 Mio. DKK. This has to be reclassified to interest expenses.

- In net income from other activities there is dividend income of 81 Mio. DKK. This has to be reclassified to interest income.

- In net income from other activities there is income from operating lease of 369 Mio. DKK. This has to be reclassified to interest income.

- All other amounts in the net income from other activities are extraordinary.

Position	Amount (DKK m)
Interest income	11,718
Interest expense	5,306
Cost of risk	−2,538
Net interest income after cost of risk	3,874
Commission income	2,102
Commission expense	343
Net commission income	1,759
Trading income	0

Position	Amount (DKK m)
Salaries	3,020
Other operating expenses	2,089
Depreciation, amortisation and impairments	424
Income before tax	100
Income tax	14
Income after tax	86
Income from discontinued operations after tax	0
Net income	86
Extraordinary income	3,003

Jyske Bank is only lightly profitable. With risk-weighted assets of 133,435 Mio. DKK (Annual report 2014, p. 122), it has a RoRWA of 86 / 133,435 = 0.06%. We have to consider the merger with BRFkredit in 2014, which might have had a big influence on the income statement.

6.28 KBC

KBC published the following data from its profit and loss account (Annual report 2014, p. 43):

Position	Amount (€m)
Interest income	8,343
Interest expense	4,266
Cost of risk	−1,714
Net interest income after cost of risk	2,363
Commission income	2,268

Position	Amount (€m)
Commission expense	798
Net commission income	1,469
Trading income	1,191
Net insurance income	289
Net income from other activities	237
Salaries	2,312
Other operating expenses	1,262
Depreciation, amortisation and impairments	269
Income before tax	1,708
Income tax	678
Income after tax	1,029
Income from discontinued operations after tax	0
Net income	1,029

We have to make the following reclassifications:

- In net income from other activities there is dividend income of 47 Mio. €. This has to be reclassified to interest income.

- All other amounts in the net income from other activities are extraordinary.

Position	Amount (€m)
Interest income	8,390
Interest expense	4,266
Cost of risk	−1,714
Net interest income after cost of risk	2,410
Commission income	2,268

Position	Amount (€m)
Commission expense	798
Net commission income	1,469
Trading income	1,191
Net insurance income	289
Salaries	2,312
Other operating expenses	1,262
Depreciation, amortisation and impairments	269
Income before tax	1,518
Income tax	678
Income after tax	839
Income from discontinued operations after tax	0
Net income	839
Extraordinary income	190

KBC is profitable. With risk-weighted assets of 91,236 Mio. € (Annual report 2014, p. 1), it has a RoRWA of 839 / 91,236 = 0.92%. The RoRWA is still quite high compared to other banks in this book, while the allocation rate is very high at 1,714 / 130,153 = 1.32%. With a *normal* allocation rate for this kind of a bank of 0.5%, KBC would reach a net income of 1,902 Mio. € and a RoRWA of 2.08%, which would be quite high.

6.29 Komercni Banka

Komercni Banka published the following data from its profit and loss account (Annual report 2014, p. 85):

Position	Amount (CZK m)
Interest income	31,222
Interest expense	9,801
Cost of risk	−1,271
Net interest income after cost of risk	20,150
Commission income	8,412
Commission expense	1,660
Net commission income	6,752
Trading income	950
Net income from other activities	1,096
Salaries	6,754
Other operating expenses	4,489
Depreciation, amortisation and impairments	1,791
Income before tax	16,030
Income tax	2,669
Income after tax	13,361
Income from discontinued operations after tax	0
Net income	13,361

We have to make the following reclassifications:

- In net income from other activities there is dividend income of 2 Mio. CZK. This has to be reclassified to interest income.

- All other amounts in the net income from other activities are extraordinary.

Position	Amount (CZK m)
Interest income	31,224
Interest expense	9,801
Cost of risk	−1,271
Net interest income after cost of risk	20,152
Commission income	8,412
Commission expense	1,660
Net commission income	6,752
Trading income	950
Salaries	6,754
Other operating expenses	4,489
Depreciation, amortisation and impairments	1,791
Income before tax	14,936
Income tax	2,669
Income after tax	12,267
Income from discontinued operations after tax	0
Net income	12,267
Extraordinary income	1,094

Komercni Banka is highly profitable. With risk-weighted assets of 384,186 Mio. CZK (Annual report 2014, p. II), it has a RoRWA of 12,267 / 384,186 = 3.19%. This bank has a low risk profile because most of the income is net interest income after cost of risk. Trading income is nearly insignificant.

6.30 Lloyds

Lloyds published the following data from its profit and loss account (Annual report 2014, p. 68):

Position	Amount (GBP m)
Interest income	19,211
Interest expense	8,551
Cost of risk	−747
Net interest income after cost of risk	9,908
Commission income	3,659
Commission expense	1,402
Net commission income	2,257
Trading income	10,159
Net income from other activities	−314
Net insurance income	−6,368
Salaries	4,745
Other operating expenses	7,205
Depreciation, amortisation and impairments	1,935
Income before tax	1,762
Income tax	263
Income after tax	1,499
Income from discontinued operations after tax	0
Net income	1,499

We have to make the following reclassification:

- All amounts in net income from other activities are extraordinary.

Position	Amount (GBP m)
Interest income	19,211
Interest expense	8,551
Cost of risk	−747
Net interest income after cost of risk	9,908
Commission income	3,659
Commission expense	1,402
Net commission income	2,257
Trading income	10,159
Net insurance income	−6,368
Salaries	4,745
Other operating expenses	7,205
Depreciation, amortisation and impairments	1,935
Income before tax	2,076
Income tax	263
Income after tax	1,813
Income from discontinued operations after tax	0
Net income	1,813
Extraordinary income	−314

Lloyds is profitable. With risk-weighted assets of 240,000 Mio. GBP (Annual report 2014, p. 2), it has a RoRWA of 1,813 / 240,000 = 0.76%. The RoRWA is quite low, especially when we consider the high trading income which is much more risky than interest income.

The high net interest income after cost of risk has to be viewed with the net insurance income. Income for the insurance holders is in the net interest income so this is shown to be much higher than it would be without the insurance business.

6.31 Mediobanca

Mediobanca published the following data from its profit and loss account (Annual report 2014/15, p. 68):

Position	Amount (€m)
Interest income	2,092
Interest expense	949
Cost of risk	−469
Net interest income after cost of risk	674
Commission income	426
Commission expense	60
Net commission income	366
Trading income	99
Net income from other activities	512
Net insurance income	24
Salaries	419
Other operating expenses	455
Depreciation, amortisation and impairments	43
Income before tax	757
Income tax	164
Income after tax	593
Income from discontinued operations after tax	0
Net income	593

We have to make the following reclassifications:

- In net income from other activities there is dividend income of 48 Mio. €. This has to be reclassified to interest income.

- In net income from other activities there is net hedging income of −1 Mio. €. This has to be reclassified to interest income.

- In net income from other activities there are net transfers to provisions of −4 Mio. €. This has to be reclassified to operating expenses.

- All amounts in the net income from other activities are extraordinary.

Position	Amount (€m)
Interest income	2,140
Interest expense	950
Cost of risk	−469
Net interest income after cost of risk	721
Commission income	426
Commission expense	60
Net commission income	366
Trading income	99
Net insurance income	24
Salaries	419
Other operating expenses	459
Depreciation, amortisation and impairments	43
Income before tax	288
Income tax	164
Income after tax	124
Income from discontinued operations after tax	0
Net income	124
Extraordinary income	469

Mediobanca is only lightly profitable. With risk-weighted assets of 59,577 Mio. € (Annual report 2014, p. 12), it has a RoRWA of 124 / 59,577 = 0.21%. One reason for the low RoRWA is the high allocation ratio of 469 / 43,201 = 1.09%. This seems to be more a cost problem rather than a credit risk problem as is the case for many of the Italian banks.

6.32 National Bank of Greece

National Bank of Greece (NBG) published the following data from its profit and loss account (Annual report 2014, p. 41):

Position	Amount (€m)
Interest income	5,285
Interest expense	2,156
Cost of risk	−2,865
Net interest income after cost of risk	264
Commission income	777
Commission expense	246
Net commission income	531
Trading income	−187
Net insurance income	86
Net income from other activities	−1
Salaries	1,163
Other operating expenses	750
Depreciation, amortisation and impairments	202
Income before tax	−1,422
Income tax	−1,528
Income after tax	106

Position	Amount (€m)
Income from discontinued operations after tax	0
Net income	106

We have to make the following reclassifications:

- All amounts in the net income from other activities are extraordinary.

Position	Amount (€m)
Interest income	5,285
Interest expense	2,156
Cost of risk	−2,865
Net interest income after cost of risk	264
Commission income	777
Commission expense	246
Net commission income	531
Trading income	−187
Net insurance income	86
Salaries	1,163
Other operating expenses	750
Depreciation, amortisation and impairments	202
Income before tax	−1,421
Income tax	−1,528
Income after tax	107
Income from discontinued operations after tax	0
Net income	107
Extraordinary income	−1

National Bank of Greece is lightly profitable, but only because of a high tax refund. With risk-weighted assets of 60,303 Mio. € (Annual report 2014, p. 12), it has a RoRWA of 107 / 60,303 = 0.18%. With a normal tax rate of 30%, National Bank of Greece would have an income after tax = net income of 70% × −1,421 Mio. € = −995 Mio. € and a RoRWA of −1.65%.

The main goal must be a reduction of the very high cost of risk, with an allocation ratio of 2,865 / 71,433 = 4.01%. With an allocation ratio of 1%, net income would be 1,127 Mio. €, giving a RoRWA of 1.87%. If NBG is able to reduce its cost of risk, it can become profitable again.

6.33 Natixis

Natixis published the following data from its profit and loss account (Annual report 2014, p. 196):

Position	Amount (€m)
Interest income	4,884
Interest expense	2,550
Cost of risk	−302
Net interest income after cost of risk	2,032
Commission income	4,475
Commission expense	1,655
Net commission income	2,820
Trading income	1,479
Net insurance income	112
Net income from other activities	834
Salaries	3,288
Other operating expenses	1,926

Position	Amount (€m)
Depreciation, amortisation and impairments	226
Income before tax	1,838
Income tax	624
Income after tax	1,214
Income from discontinued operations after tax	0
Net income	1,214

We have to make the following reclassifications:

- In net income from other activities there is dividend income of 172 Mio. €. This has to be reclassified to interest income.

- All other amounts in the net income from other activities are extraordinary.

Position	Amount (€m)
Interest income	5,056
Interest expense	2,550
Cost of risk	−302
Net interest income after cost of risk	2,204
Commission income	4,475
Commission expense	1,655
Net commission income	2,820
Trading income	1,479
Net insurance income	112
Salaries	3,288
Other operating expenses	1,926
Depreciation, amortisation and impairments	226

Position	Amount (€m)
Income before tax	1,176
Income tax	624
Income after tax	552
Income from discontinued operations after tax	0
Net income	552
Extraordinary income	662

Natixis is lightly profitable. With risk-weighted assets of 115,200 Mio. € (Annual report 2014, p. 8), it has a RoRWA of 552 / 115,200 = 0.48%. The RoRWA is much too low for an investment bank like Natixis.

6.34 Nordea Bank

Nordea Bank published the following data from its profit and loss account (Annual report 2014, p. 196):

Position	Amount (€m)
Interest income	9,995
Interest expense	4,513
Cost of risk	−534
Net interest income after cost of risk	4,948
Commission income	3,799
Commission expense	957
Net commission income	2,842
Trading income	1,425
Net income from other activities	475

Position	Amount (€m)
Salaries	3,149
Other operating expenses	1,635
Depreciation, amortisation and impairments	582
Income before tax	4,324
Income tax	953
Income after tax	3,371
Income from discontinued operations after tax	−39
Net income	3,332

We have to make the following reclassification:

- All amounts in the net income from other activities are extraordinary.

Position	Amount (€m)
Interest income	9,995
Interest expense	4,513
Cost of risk	−534
Net interest income after cost of risk	4,948
Commission income	3,799
Commission expense	957
Net commission income	2,842
Trading income	1,425
Salaries	3,149
Other operating expenses	1,635
Depreciation, amortisation and impairments	582
Income before tax	3,829

Position	Amount (€m)
Income tax	953
Income after tax	2,896
Income from discontinued operations after tax	−39
Net income	2,857
Net income from other activities	475

Nordea Bank is highly profitable. With risk-weighted assets of 220,413 Mio. € (Annual report 2014, p. 8), it has a RoRWA of 2,857 / 220,413 = 1.30%. With this RoRWA, Nordea is one of the strongest banks in Europe. From the risk profile, Nordea is a low-risk bank. For that, the RoRWA is fine.

6.35 Raiffeisen

Raiffeisen published the following data from its profit and loss account (Annual report 2014, p. 92):

Position	Amount (€m)
Interest income	5,616
Interest expense	1,827
Cost of risk	−1,716
Net interest income after cost of risk	2,073
Commission income	2,007
Commission expense	421
Net commission income	1,586
Trading income	−30
Net income from other activities	−583

Position	Amount (€m)
Salaries	1,450
Other operating expenses	1,193
Depreciation, amortisation and impairments	381
Income before tax	23
Income tax	486
Income after tax	−463
Income from discontinued operations after tax	0
Net income	−463

We have to make the following reclassifications:

- In costs of risk there is an amount of +68 Mio. € from the sale of loans. This has to be reclassified as extraordinary income.

- In other income there is an amount of −262 Mio. € for other taxes. This has to be reclassified as other operating expenses.

- In other income there is an amount of −25 Mio. € for other provisions. This has to be reclassified as other operating expenses.

- All amounts in the net income from other activities are extraordinary.

Position	Amount (€m)
Interest income	5,616
Interest expense	1,827
Cost of risk	−1,784
Net interest income after cost of risk	2,073
Commission income	2,007
Commission expense	421
Net commission income	1,586

Position	Amount (€m)
Trading income	-30
Salaries	1,450
Other operating expenses	1,480
Depreciation, amortisation and impairments	381
Income before tax	251
Income tax	486
Income after tax	-235
Income from discontinued operations after tax	0
Net income	-235
Extraordinary income	-228

Raiffeisen is lightly unprofitable, but this is because of a much too high income tax compared to the income before tax. With risk-weighted assets of 68,721 Mio. € (Annual report 2014, p. 103), it has a RoRWA of −235 / 68,721 = −0.34%. With a normal tax rate of 30%, the net income would be 70% × 251 Mio. € = 176 Mio. € and the RoRWA = 0.26%. This very low RoRWA mostly depends on the very high allocation rate of 1,784 / 93,499 = 1.91%. With an allocation rate of 1%, the net income would already be 1,025 Mio. € and the RoRWA = 1.49%.

Raiffeisen is mostly working in Eastern Europe with a higher risk profile than other banks. For this, it needs a higher RoRWA.

6.36 Royal Bank of Scotland

Royal Bank of Scotland published the following data from its profit and loss account (Annual report 2014, p. 342):

Position	Amount (GBP m)
Interest income	13,079
Interest expense	3,821
Cost of risk	1,352
Net interest income after cost of risk	10,610
Commission income	4,414
Commission expense	875
Net commission income	3,539
Trading income	1,285
Net income from other activities	545
Salaries	5,757
Other operating expenses	6,649
Depreciation, amortisation and impairments	930
Income before tax	2,643
Income tax	1,909
Income after tax	734
Income from discontinued operations after tax	−3,445
Net income	−2,711

We have to make the following reclassifications:

- In net income from other activities there is operating lease income of 380 Mio. GBP. This has to be reclassified to interest income.

- All amounts in the net income from other activities are extraordinary.

Position	Amount (GBP m)
Interest income	13,459
Interest expense	3,821
Cost of risk	1,352
Net interest income after cost of risk	10,990
Commission income	4,414
Commission expense	875
Net commission income	3,539
Trading income	1,285
Salaries	5,757
Other operating expenses	6,649
Depreciation, amortisation and impairments	930
Income before tax	2,478
Income tax	1,909
Income after tax	569
Income from discontinued operations after tax	−3,445
Net income	−2,876
Extraordinary income	165

Royal Bank of Scotland is, according to the income after tax, profitable. With risk-weighted assets of 355,900 Mio. GBP (Annual report 2014, p. 127), it has a RoRWA of 569 / 355,900 = 0.16%. Unfortunately, the income after tax is only positive because of a positive cost of risk. Royal Bank of Scotland has had higher earnings in cost of risk because not all impairments from the past had to be used. This is a one-time effect.

Normally, the cost of risk will always be negative. With an allocation ratio of 0.5%, Royal Bank of Scotland would have cost of risk of 0.5% × 421,973 Mio. GBP = 2,110 Mio. GBP, so the income before tax would be −984 Mio. GBP instead of a positive value.

In fact, Royal Bank of Scotland is still highly unprofitable with a RoRWA based on the allocation ratio of 0.5% of −0.28%.

6.37 SEB

SEB published the following data from its profit and loss account (Annual report 2014, p. 64):

Position	Amount (SEK m)
Interest income	48,624
Interest expense	28,681
Cost of risk	−1,324
Net interest income after cost of risk	18,619
Commission income	21,418
Commission expense	5,112
Net commission income	16,306
Trading income	2,921
Net insurance income	3,345
Net income from other activities	4,300
Salaries	13,760
Other operating expenses	6,310
Depreciation, amortisation and impairments	2,073
Income before tax	23,348
Income tax	4,129
Income after tax	19,219

Position	Amount (SEK m)
Income from discontinued operations after tax	0
Net income	19,219

We have to make the following reclassifications:

- In other income there is an amount of +78 Mio. SEK for dividends income. This has to be reclassified as interest income.

- All other amounts in the net income from other activities are extraordinary.

Position	Amount (SEK m)
Interest income	48,702
Interest expense	28,681
Cost of risk	−1,324
Net interest income after cost of risk	18,697
Commission income	21,418
Commission expense	5,112
Net commission income	16,306
Trading income	2,921
Net insurance income	3,345
Salaries	13,760
Other operating expenses	6,310
Depreciation, amortisation and impairments	2,073
Income before tax	19,126
Income tax	4,129
Income after tax	14,997
Income from discontinued operations after tax	0

Position	Amount (SEK m)
Net income	14,997
Extraordinary income	4,222

SEB is strongly profitable. With risk-weighted assets of 616,531 Mio. SEK (Annual report 2014, p. 120), it has a RoRWA of 14,997 / 616,531 = 2.43%. The income comes mostly from net interest income after cost of risk and net commission income, so the risk profile from the income statement view is low risk.

6.38 Société Générale

Société Générale published the following data from its profit and loss account (Annual report 2014, p. 64):

Position	Amount (€m)
Interest income	24,532
Interest expense	14,533
Cost of risk	−2,967
Net interest income after cost of risk	7,032
Commission income	9,159
Commission expense	2,684
Net commission income	6,475
Trading income	4,481
Net income from other activities	1,971
Salaries	9,049
Other operating expenses	6,060
Depreciation, amortisation and impairments	907

Position	Amount (€m)
Income before tax	4,375
Income tax	1,384
Income after tax	2,991
Income from discontinued operations after tax	0
Net income	2,991

We have to make the following reclassifications:

- In other income there is an amount of +428 Mio. € for net insurance income. This has to be reclassified as operating income.

- All other amounts in the net income from other activities are extraordinary.

Position	Amount (€m)
Interest income	24,532
Interest expense	14,533
Cost of risk	−2,967
Net interest income after cost of risk	7,032
Commission income	9,159
Commission expense	2,684
Net commission income	6,475
Trading income	4,481
Net insurance income	428
Salaries	9,049
Other operating expenses	6,060
Depreciation, amortisation and impairments	907
Income before tax	2,832

Position	Amount (€m)
Income tax	1,384
Income after tax	1,448
Income from discontinued operations after tax	0
Net income	1,448
Extraordinary income	1,543

Société Générale is profitable. It has risk-weighted assets of 353,196 Mio. € (Pillar 3 report 2014, p. 26), it has a RoRWA of 1,448 / 353,196 = 0.41%. For its risks – high trading income – the RoRWA is much too low.

6.39 Standard Chartered

Standard Chartered published the following data from its profit and loss account (Annual report 2014, p. 225):

Position	Amount (US-$ m)
Interest income	16,984
Interest expense	5,981
Cost of risk	−2,141
Net interest income after cost of risk	8,862
Commission income	4,651
Commission expense	472
Net commission income	4,179
Trading income	1,896
Net income from other activities	343

Position	Amount (US-$ m)
Salaries	6,788
Other operating expenses	3,618
Depreciation, amortisation and impairments	639
Income before tax	4,235
Income tax	1,530
Income after tax	2,705
Income from discontinued operations after tax	0
Net income	2,705

We have to make the following reclassifications:

- In net income from other activities there is dividend income of 97 Mio. US-$. This has to be reclassified to interest income.

- In net income from other activities there is operating lease income of 562 Mio. US-$. This has to be reclassified to interest income.

- All other amounts in the net income from other activities are extraordinary.

Position	Amount (US-$ m)
Interest income	17,643
Interest expense	5,981
Cost of risk	−2,141
Net interest income after cost of risk	8,862
Commission income	4,651
Commission expense	472
Net commission income	4,179
Trading income	1,896
Salaries	6,788

Position	Amount (US-$ m)
Other operating expenses	3,618
Depreciation, amortisation and impairments	639
Income before tax	4,551
Income tax	1,530
Income after tax	3,021
Income from discontinued operations after tax	0
Net income	3,021
Extraordinary income	–316

Standard Chartered is profitable. With risk-weighted assets of 341,648 Mio. US-$ (Annual report 2014, p. 39), it has a RoRWA of 3,021 / 341,648 = 0.88%. The RoRWA is not very high, but it is positive that the income comes mostly from net interest income after cost of risk and net commission income, while the trading income is quite low.

6.40 Svenska Handelsbanken

Svenska Handelsbanken published the following data from its the profit and loss account (Annual report 2014, p. 67):

Position	Amount (SEK m)
Interest income	50,899
Interest expense	23,655
Cost of risk	–1,781
Net interest income after cost of risk	25,463
Commission income	10,143
Commission expense	1,587

Position	Amount (SEK m)
Net commission income	8,556
Trading income	1,777
Net insurance income	165
Net income from other activities	578
Salaries	11,766
Other operating expenses	5,099
Depreciation, amortisation and impairments	462
Income before tax	19,212
Income tax	4,069
Income after tax	15,143
Income from discontinued operations after tax	41
Net income	15,184

We have to make the following reclassifications:

- In other income there is an amount of +251 Mio. SEK for dividends income. This has to be reclassified as interest income.

- All other amounts in the net income from other activities are extraordinary.

Position	Amount (SEK m)
Interest income	51,150
Interest expense	23,655
Cost of risk	−1,781
Net interest income after cost of risk	25,714
Commission income	10,143
Commission expense	1,587

Position	Amount (SEK m)
Net commission income	8,556
Trading income	1,777
Net insurance income	165
Salaries	11,766
Other operating expenses	5,099
Depreciation, amortisation and impairments	462
Income before tax	18,885
Income tax	4,069
Income after tax	14,816
Income from discontinued operations after tax	41
Net income	14,857
Extraordinary income	327

Svenska Handelsbanken is strongly profitable. With risk-weighted assets of 616,531 Mio. SEK (Annual report 2014, p. 145), it has a RoRWA of 14,857 / 480,388 = 3.09%. The income comes mostly from net interest income after cost of risk, so the risk profile from the income statement view is extremely low risk.

6.41 Swedbank

Swedbank published the following data from its profit and loss account (Annual report 2014, p. 62):

Position	Amount (SEK m)
Interest income	41,052
Interest expense	18,410

Position	Amount (SEK m)
Cost of risk	–419
Net interest income after cost of risk	22,223
Commission income	16,252
Commission expense	5,048
Net commission income	11,204
Trading income	1,986
Net insurance income	581
Net income from other activities	2,634
Salaries	10,259
Other operating expenses	6,625
Depreciation, amortisation and impairments	718
Income before tax	21,026
Income tax	4,301
Income after tax	16,725
Income from discontinued operations after tax	–262
Net income	16,463

We have to make the following reclassifications:

- All amounts in the net income from other activities are extraordinary.

Position	Amount (SEK m)
Interest income	41,052
Interest expense	18,410
Cost of risk	–419
Net interest income after cost of risk	22,223

Position	Amount (SEK m)
Commission income	16,252
Commission expense	5,048
Net commission income	11,204
Trading income	1,986
Net insurance income	581
Salaries	10,259
Other operating expenses	6,625
Depreciation, amortisation and impairments	718
Income before tax	18,392
Income tax	4,301
Income after tax	14,091
Income from discontinued operations after tax	−262
Net income	13,829
Extraordinary income	2,634

Swedbank, like all Swedish banks, is strongly profitable. With risk-weighted assets of 414,214 Mio. SEK (Annual report 2014, p. 97), it has a RoRWA of 13,829 / 414,214 = 3.34%. The income comes mostly from net interest income after cost of risk, so the risk profile from the income statement view is extremely low risk.

6.42 Sydbank

Sydbank published the following data from its profit and loss account (Annual report 2014, p. 62):

Position	Amount (DKK m)
Interest income	3,341
Interest expense	599
Cost of risk	−692
Net interest income after cost of risk	2,050
Commission income	1,750
Commission expense	238
Net commission income	1,512
Trading income	391
Net income from other activities	40
Salaries	1,564
Other operating expenses	1,047
Depreciation, amortisation and impairments	96
Income before tax	1,329
Income tax	277
Income after tax	1,052
Income from discontinued operations after tax	0
Net income	1,052

We have to make the following reclassifications:

- All amounts in the net income from other activities are extraordinary.

Position	Amount (DKK m)
Interest income	3,341
Interest expense	599
Cost of risk	−692
Net interest income after cost of risk	2,050
Commission income	1,750
Commission expense	238
Net commission income	1,512
Trading income	391
Salaries	1,564
Other operating expenses	1,047
Depreciation, amortisation and impairments	96
Income before tax	1,289
Income tax	277
Income after tax	1,012
Income from discontinued operations after tax	0
Net income	1,012
Extraordinary income	40

Sydbank is profitable. With risk-weighted assets of 72,500 Mio. DKK (Annual report 2014, p. 16), it has a RoRWA of 1,012 / 72,500 = 1.40%. The income comes mostly from net interest income after cost of risk and net commission income, so the risk profile from the income statement view is low risk.

The net income is mostly influenced by the cost of risk. In 2014, the allocation ratio was 692 / 75,342 = 0.92%, but in 2013 it was 1,861 / 71,477 = 2.60%. Even with this very high allocation ratio, Sydbank was still profitable.

6.43 UBS

UBS published the following data from its profit and loss account (Annual report 2014, p. 436):

Position	Amount (CHF m)
Interest income	13,194
Interest expense	6,639
Cost of risk	−78
Net interest income after cost of risk	6,477
Commission income	18,940
Commission expense	1,863
Net commission income	17,076
Trading income	3,842
Net income from other activities	632
Salaries	15,280
Other operating expenses	9,387
Depreciation, amortisation and impairments	900
Income before tax	2,461
Income tax	−1,180
Income after tax	3,640
Income from discontinued operations after tax	0
Net income	3,640

We have to make the following reclassifications:

- In interest income there is an amount of +3,196 Mio. CHF and in interest expenses an amount of −1,804 Mio. CHF for trading business. This has to be reclassified as trading income.

- All amounts in the net income from other activities are extraordinary.

Position	Amount (CHF m)
Interest income	9,998
Interest expense	4,835
Cost of risk	−78
Net interest income after cost of risk	5,085
Commission income	18,940
Commission expense	1,863
Net commission income	17,076
Trading income	5,234
Salaries	15,280
Other operating expenses	9,387
Depreciation, amortisation and impairments	900
Income before tax	1,829
Income tax	−1,180
Income after tax	3,008
Income from discontinued operations after tax	0
Net income	3,008
Extraordinary income	632

UBS is profitable. With risk-weighted assets of 220,877 Mio. CHF (Annual report 2014, p. 291), it has a RoRWA of 3,008 / 220,877 = 1.36%. But it has to be mentioned that UBS got a tax refund in 2014. With a normal tax rate of 30%, net income would have been 70% × 1,829 Mio CHF = 1,280 Mio. CHF and the RoRWA = 0.58%.

UBS provides wealth management, asset management and investment banking. For this kind of business, the RoRWA is much too low. Lower risk income like net interest income after cost of risk is less important for UBS than trade income. This makes the risk profile from the income statement a high-risk bank.

6.44 UniCredit

UniCredit published the following data from its profit and loss account (Annual report 2014, p. 64):

Position	Amount (€m)
Interest income	21,742
Interest expense	9,680
Cost of risk	−4,178
Net interest income after cost of risk	7,883
Commission income	9,070
Commission expense	1,585
Net commission income	7,485
Trading income	636
Net income from other activities	2,441
Salaries	8,204
Other operating expenses	5,569
Depreciation, amortisation and impairments	1,193
Income before tax	3,679
Income tax	1,167
Income after tax	2,512
Income from discontinued operations after tax	−124
Net income	2,388

We have to make the following reclassifications:

- In other income there is dividend income of 402 Mio. €. This has to be reclassified as interest income.

- In other income there are fair value adjustments in hedge accounting of −9 Mio. €. This has to be reclassified as interest income.

- In other income there is net provisions for risks and charges of −384 Mio. €. This has to be reclassified as operating expenses.

- All other amounts in the net income from other activities are extraordinary.

Position	Amount (€m)
Interest income	21,144
Interest expense	9,689
Cost of risk	−4,178
Net interest income after cost of risk	8,294
Commission income	9,070
Commission expense	1,585
Net commission income	7,485
Trading income	636
Salaries	8,204
Other operating expenses	5,953
Depreciation, amortisation and impairments	1,193
Income before tax	1,247
Income tax	1,167
Income after tax	80
Income from discontinued operations after tax	−124
Net income	−44
Extraordinary income	2,432

UniCredit is lightly unprofitable, but only because of the income tax. With a normal tax rate of 30%, UniCredit would have income after tax of 70% × 1,247 Mio. € = 873 Mio. €. With risk-weighted assets of 409,223 Mio. € (Annual report 2014, p. 472), it has a RoRWA of 873 / 409,223 = 0.21%. The RoRWA is so low because of quite a high allocation ratio of 4,178 / 539,299 = 0.77%. For an Italian bank in 2014 the allocation ratio is low, but still too high to have a better performance.

With an allocation ratio of 0.5%, income after tax would be 2,355 Mio. € and the RoRWA = 0.58%: this is still too low. UniCredit has, like the other Italian banks, not only a credit risk problem but also high costs that are too high.

6.45 UBI Unione di Banche

UBI Unione di Banche published the following data from its profit and loss account (Annual report 2014, p. 86):

Position	Amount (€m)
Interest income	3,015
Interest expense	1,197
Cost of risk	−929
Net interest income after cost of risk	889
Commission income	1,403
Commission expense	177
Net commission income	1,227
Trading income	63
Net income from other activities	−449
Salaries	1,413
Other operating expenses	860
Depreciation, amortisation and impairments	233

Position	Amount (€m)
Income before tax	−776
income tax	−72
Income after tax	−704
Income from discontinued operations after tax	0
Net income	−704

We have to make the following reclassifications:

- In other income there is dividend income of 10 Mio. €. This has to be reclassified as interest income.

- In other income there are fair value adjustments in hedge accounting of −11 Mio. €. This has to be reclassified as interest income.

- In other income there are net provisions for risks and charges of −9 Mio. €. This has to be reclassified as operating expenses.

- All other amounts in the net income from other activities are extraordinary.

Position	Amount (€m)
Interest income	3,025
Interest expense	1,208
Cost of risk	−929
Net interest income after cost of risk	888
Commission income	1,403
Commission expense	177
Net commission income	1,227
Trading income	63
Salaries	1,413
Other operating expenses	869

Position	Amount (€m)
Depreciation, amortisation and impairments	233
Income before tax	−337
Income tax	−72
Income after tax	−265
Income from discontinued operations after tax	0
Net income	−265
Extraordinary income	−439

UBI Unione di Banche is lightly unprofitable. With risk-weighted assets of 61,763 Mio. € (Annual report 2014, p. 12), it has a RoRWA of −265 / 61,763 = −0.43%. The RoRWA is so low because of a quite high allocation ratio of 929 / 88,985 = 1.04%. For an Italian bank in 2014, the allocation ratio is low, but still too high to have a better performance.

With an allocation ratio of 0.5%, income after tax would be 219 Mio. € and the RoRWA = 0.25%: still much too low! UBI Unione di Banche has, like the other Italian banks, not only a credit risk problem but also costs that are too high.

6.46 Conclusions about income statement analysis

The following table shows the banks with their RoRWA for the year 2014 with their home country and the rank after RoRWA. The banks are ordered by RoRWA rank.

Bank	RoRWA	Home Country	Rank
Swedbank	3.34%	Sweden	1
Komercni Banka	3.19%	Czech Rep.	2

Bank	RoRWA	Home Country	Rank
Svenska Handelsbanken	3.09%	Sweden	3
SEB	2.43%	Sweden	4
Julius Bär	1.85%	Switzerland	5
DNB	1.70%	Norway	6
Sydbank	1.40%	Denmark	7
Nordea Bank	1.30%	Sweden	8
Danske Bank	1.26%	Denmark	9
Bankinter	1.00%	Spain	10
KBC	0.92%	Belgium	11
Standard Chartered	0.88%	UK	12
Banco Santander	0.81%	Spain	13
HSBC	0.80%	UK	14
Bankia	0.76%	Spain	15
Lloyds	0.76%	UK	15
BNP Paribas	0.73%	France	17
Crédit Agricole	0.67%	France	18
Bank of Ireland	0.64%	Ireland	19
BBVA	0.59%	Spain	20
UBS	0.58%	Switzerland	21
Erste Group Bank	0.48%	Austria	22
Natixis	0.48%	France	22
Société Générale	0.41%	France	24
Banco Popular	0.41%	Spain	24
Caixabank	0.33%	Spain	26
Barclays	0.25%	UK	27
Mediobanca	0.21%	Italy	28

Bank	RoRWA	Home Country	Rank
UniCredit	0.21%	Italy	28
National Bank of Greece	0.18%	Greece	30
Royal Bank of Scotland	0.16%	UK	31
Jyske Bank	0.06%	Denmark	32
Credit Suisse	0.03%	Switzerland	33
Deutsche Bank	0.02%	Germany	34
Commerzbank	−0.10%	Germany	35
Intesa Sanpaolo	−0.10%	Italy	35
Banca Popolare di Sondrio	−0.26%	Italy	37
Raiffeisen	−0.34%	Austria	38
UBI Unione di Banche	−0.43%	Italy	39
Banca Popolare dell'Emilia Romagna	−0.61%	Italy	40
Banco Comercial Portugues	−0.79%	Portugal	41
Banco de Sabadell	−1.82%	Spain	42
Banca Carige	−2.67%	Italy	43
Banco Popolare	−4.34%	Italy	44
Banca Monte dei Paschi	−6.89%	Italy	45

We can find two interesting results from the RoRWA analysis. First, smaller banks can achieve a much higher RoRWA than bigger banks. The seven banks with the highest RoRWAs are much smaller than the big banks like HSBC (rank 14), Deutsche Bank (rank 34), UBS (rank 21) or BNP Paribas (rank 17). We find proof that size is not a benefit at all for a bank, but in fact there are huge diseconomies of scale.

Second, there are big differences in the home country results. The following table shows the results for the different home countries. The countries are ordered by the average RoRWA rank.

Country	Number of banks	Average RoRWA	Rank
Czech Rep.	1	3.19%	1
Sweden	4	2.54%	2
Norway	1	1.70%	3
Belgium	1	0.92%	4
Switzerland	3	0.82%	5
Denmark	3	0.77%	6
Ireland	1	0.64%	7
France	4	0.58%	8
UK	5	0.57%	9
Spain	7	0.30%	10
Austria	2	0.07%	11
Germany	2	−0.04%	12
Portugal	1	−0.79%	13
Italy	9	−1.65%	14

Again, smaller countries like Sweden, Czech Republic, Norway and Belgium have better results than big countries like France, Spain, Italy and Germany. In combination with what we have seen above about the size of a bank, we can say again that smaller banks can be more profitable than big banks.

In Italy, most of the banks are unprofitable. This seems to be a country-specific problem and not a bank-specific problem. In other southern European countries, which also got hit very hard by the crisis, such as Spain, the results are much better than in Italy.

Furthermore, for many Italian banks not only was a credit risk problem identified but a cost problem too. These banks have to go through a deep restructuring before they will be able to become profitable again.

7. Equity Analysis

Equity is the most important number in banking supervision. The supervisory rules for solvency ratio and several other ratios are used to limit the risk-weighted assets of a bank. In contrast to an industrial company, a bank always needs equity to run its business. An industrial company can run its business with negative equity, but for a bank this is impossible.

Equity in general and tier 1 capital specifically are the numbers that restrict bank business. Banks can decide to use a portion of equity for one loan, one security or whatever else. When this loan is repaid, the equity can be used again. Until it is repaid, the equity is fixed in this loan. An industrial company can always borrow money from banks – as long as banks lend it money, it can buy new assets. This is precisely what a bank cannot do.

In fact, we can calculate a RoRWA for each bit of business a bank is doing, and – because of the restricting influence of the equity on the risk-weighted assets – even a return on equity for every bit of business a bank is doing.

It is possible to discuss at length the advantages and disadvantages of the way risk-weighted assets and the tier 1 capital are calculated. However, this book is about analysis and not about banking supervision, so I do not enter into this discussion. As long as banking supervision calculates risk-weighted assets in this way, it is the way the analyst must look at equity too.

Tier 1 capital has two ingredients: Common Equity Tier 1 (CET 1) and Additional Tier 1 (AT 1). Tier 1 capital must be higher than 6% of risk-weighted assets, while CET 1 alone must be higher than 4.5% of risk-weighted assets. Additionally, banks must hold 2.5% of risk-weighted assets as a capital conservation buffer, under CET 1. The capital conservation buffer can be breached by losses in times of crisis. In this case, banks are not allowed to pay dividends and so on until the capital conservation buffer is complete again.

Local authorities can also activate a countercyclical buffer of 0%-2.5% or even more, if national law allows this (for example German BaFin can even make a higher buffer than 2.5%). This amount has to be fulfilled through CET 1 capital too. The countercyclical buffer will be activated when the credit growth is too high in a country. Implemented by most countries on 1/1/2016, Sweden and Norway both activated a countercyclical buffer of 1.5% for 2017, so banks there have to fulfil a CET 1 ratio of 8.5%. Additionally, Hong Kong set the countercyclical buffer to 1.25%.

The above capital requirements are the same for all banks in a country. For global systemically important banks (G-SIBs), the Financial Stability Board adds additional capital requirements. The following banks from the sample used in this book have to fulfil this kind of additional capital requirement:

Bank	CET 1 additional
HSBC	2.5%
Barclays	2.0%
BNP Paribas	2.0%
Deutsche Bank	2.0%
Credit Suisse	1.5%
Royal Bank of Scotland	1.5%
Banco Santander	1.0%
BBVA	1.0%
Crédit Agricole	1.0%

Bank	CET 1 additional
Nordea	1.0%
Société Générale	1.0%
Standard Chartered	1.0%
UBS	1.0%
UniCredit	1.0%

In addition, national law can differ from the common rules mentioned above. Switzerland, for example, has much higher capital requirements for systemically relevant banks than other countries.

The CET 1 consists mainly of shareholders' equity and non-controlling interests, while intangible assets and deferred tax assets that rely on future profitability – in particular – have to be subtracted from these amounts. Many other corrections have to be done to calculate CET 1 as well, but the main positions which are normally relevant are those mentioned here.

AT 1 consists, for example, of preference shares or hybrid capital. Such hybrid capital normally contains the rule to strengthen the equity in cases where the tier 1 capital ratio falls under a special limit. For Deutsche Bank, for example, the limit is 5.125% (Annual report 2014, p. 467).

The main rate for banking supervision is the solvency ratio. The solvency ratio has to be 8% of risk-weighted assets without the conservation buffer and 10.5% with it. Additionally, the countercyclical buffer and the rates for global systematically important banks described above have to be added.

The basis for the solvency ratio is the total regulatory capital. Total regulatory capital is the tier 1 capital and the tier 2 capital. Tier 2 capital is, for example, subordinated debt.

In addition to the capital requirement ratio based on the risk-weighted assets, banks have to fulfil the leverage ratio. The leverage ratio is the quotient between CET 1 and the total assets corrected by regulatory adjustments. Adjustments are, for example, the adding of the off-balance-sheet commitments and guarantees. The minimum leverage ratio from the regulatory point of view is 3%.

Both the leverage ratio and solvency ratio have advantages and disadvantages. Just to present a couple of arguments on this matter:

- The leverage ratio penalises banks which take less credit risk because all assets are treated the same. Banks may therefore tend to do more risky business.

- The solvency ratio uses risk weights to calculate risk-weighted assets. The risk weights were wrong during the financial crisis.

Normally, banks will only get one ratio near to its target, while the other ratio will be far away from its target. Actually, because these rules are new, many banks have needed to increase their capital or decrease their credit risks respective to total assets in order to fulfil the ratios. From the beginning of the financial crisis up to 2011, the following banks from the sample in this book had to increase their capital:[5]

Bank	Capital increase (€m)
Lloyds	15,900
Deutsche Bank	10,200
BBVA	5,100
Société Générale	4,800
BNP Paribas	4,300
UniCredit	4,000
Standard Chartered	3,900
Banco Popolare	2,000

---

5. Statista.com (bit.ly/2f58u6k).

The quotient between risk-weighted assets and total assets corrected by regulatory adjustments shows if a bank's decisive rule is the solvency ratio or the leverage ratio.

The following applies:

- If risk-weighted assets / corrected total assets > 3/7 then CET 1 ratio is decisive.
- If risk-weighted assets / corrected total assets < 3/7 then leverage ratio is decisive.
- If risk-weighted assets / corrected total assets = 3/7 then both ratios are equally decisive.

These formulas are for non G-SIB banks. For G-SIB banks, the denominator has to be increased by the additional capital requirement.

Example

Deutsche Bank has an additional CET 1 requirement of 2%. The ratio for Deutsche Bank is:

- If risk-weighted assets / corrected total assets > 3/9 then CET 1 ratio is decisive.
- If risk-weighted assets / corrected total assets < 3/9 then leverage ratio is decisive.
- If risk-weighted assets / corrected total assets = 3/9 then both ratios are equally decisive.

Example

Deutsche Bank reports the following data (Annual report 2014, pp. 277, 284):

Risk-weighted assets: 396,648 Mio. €

Corrected total assets: 1,445,000 Mio. €

risk-weighted assets / corrected total assets = 396,648 / 1,445,000 = 0.2745 < 0.33

This means the leverage ratio is decisive for Deutsche Bank.

Most banks have a ratio between risk-weighted assets and corrected total assets over 3/7 (or their specific value because of G-SIB), so the CET 1 ratio will be decisive for them.

The limiting factor for bank management is either risk-weighted assets or corrected total assets. The main problem for bank management is that there is a different method of management depending on whether the bank follows the total assets or the risk-weighted assets.

Example

A bank wants to invest in treasuries. Its limiting factor is the risk-weighted assets. The treasuries are included in risk-weighted assets with a weight factor of 0%, so the investment has no influence on the risk-weighted assets and the CET 1 ratio. Following the risk-weighted assets, treasuries have no influence on the risk-weighted assets and therefore no equity is needed for them.

Example

A bank wants to invest in treasuries. Its limiting factor is the corrected total assets. Because the treasuries are included fully in corrected total assets, an equity of minimum 3% of their value is used.

The examples above show how much influence banking regulation has on bank management. In fact, for banks whose limiting factor is the leverage ratio, return-on-assets (ROA) is the better return-on number to use than return on risk-weighted assets (RoRWA). To compare banks, RoRWA is still used for all banks in this book.

Example

HSBC has an additional CET 1 requirement of 2.5%. The ratio for HSBC is:

If risk-weighted assets / corrected total assets > 3/9.5 then CET 1 ratio is decisive.

If risk-weighted assets / corrected total assets < 3/9.5 then leverage ratio is decisive.

If risk-weighted assets / corrected total assets = 3/9.5 then both ratios are equally decisive.

HSBC reports the following data (Annual report 2014, p. 31):

Risk-weighted assets	1,220,000 Mio. US-$
Corrected total assets	2,953,000 Mio. US-$

risk-weighted assets / corrected total assets = 1,220,000 / 2,953,000 = 0.413 > 0.3158

This means the CET 1 ratio is decisive for HSBC.

For analysis, we have to look for both numbers – CET 1 ratio and leverage ratio. The following table contains the CET 1 ratio, solvency ratio and additionally risk-weighted assets and total assets for the banks used in this book.

It has to be mentioned that the leverage ratio will be in banking supervision use from 2018, so not all banks have published this data so far. Additionally, full CET 1 rules will be in use from 2018. I have used here the data based on the 2018 rules, if available. If not, data is marked with a * in the table.

Name	CET 1 ratio	Solvency ratio	RWA	Total assets	RWA / Total assets
Banca Carige	8.4%*	11.2%*	20,474	25,973	78.8%
Banca Monte dei Paschi	8.7%*	13.0%*	76,220	179,574	42.4%
Banco Bilbao Vizcaya Argentaria (BBVA)	10.4%	15.0%*	350,802	631,942	55.5%

Name	CET 1 ratio	Solvency ratio	RWA	Total assets	RWA / Total assets
Banco Comercial Portugues	8.9%	13.7%*	42,376	76,361	55.5%
Banco de Sabadell	11.7%*	12.8%*	60,071	163,346	36.8%
Banco Popolare	11.9%*	14.6%	47,987	123,082	39.0%
Banco Popular	11.5%*	12.0%	80,113	161,456	49.6%
Banco Santander	9.7%	13.3*	585,243	1,266,296	46.2%
Bank of Ireland	9.3%	18.3%*	51,600	129,800	39.8%
Bankia	12.3%*	13.8%*	88,565	233,649	37.9%
Bankinter	11.9%*	13.1%*	25,704	60,012	42.8%
Barclays	10.3%	16.5%*	442,471	1,357,906	32.6%
Banca Popolare di Sondrio	9.8%*	11.3%*	21,338	32,573	65.5%
Banca Popolare dell'Emilia Romagna	11.3%*	12.2%*	40,692	60,653	67.1%
BNP Paribas	10.3%	12.6%	614,449	2,077,759	29.6%
Caixabank	13.1%*	16.2%*	139,519	338,623	41.2%
Commerzbank	11.7%*	14.6%*	215,200	557,600	38.6%
Credit Suisse	17.1%*	20.8%	291,410	921,462	31.6%
Crédit Agricole	13.1%	16.7%	494,934	1,762,763	28.1%
Danske Bank	15.1%*	19.3%	866,000	3,453,015	25.1%
Deutsche Bank	11.7%	16.0%	393,969	1,708,703	23.1%
DNB	12.7%*	15.2%*	1,120,659	2,649,341	42.3%
Erste Group Bank	10.6%*	15.6%*	101,870	196,287	51.9%
HSBC	11.1%	15.6%*	1,219,765	2,634,139	46.3%

Name	CET 1 ratio	Solvency ratio	RWA	Total assets	RWA / Total assets
Intesa Sanpaolo	13.5%*	17.2%*	269,790	646,427	41.7%
Julius Bär	22.0%*	23.4%*	16,978	82,234	20.6%
Jyske Bank	15.3%*	16.4%*	176,433	541,679	32.6%
KBC	14.3%	18.3%*	91,236	245,174	37.2%
Komercni Banka	16.4%*	16.4%*	384,186	953,261	40.3%
Lloyds	12.8%*	22.0%*	240,000	854,896	28.1%
Mediobanca	12.0%*	14.9%*	59,577	70,711	84.3%
National Bank of Greece	13.6%*	13.7%*	60,303	115,464	52.2%
Natixis	11.4%*	13.8%*	115,200	590,400	19.5%
Nordea Bank	15.7%*	20.7%*	145,000	669,342	21.7%
Raiffeisen	10.9%	16.0%	68,721	121,624	56.5%
Royal Bank of Scotland	11.2%*	13.7%*	355,900	1,050,763	33.9%
SEB	16.3%*	22.2%*	616,531	2,641,246	23.3%
Société Générale	10.1%*	14.3%*	353,200	1,308,170	27.0%
Standard Chartered	10.7%	16.7%	341,648	725,914	47.1%
Svenska Handelsbanken	20.4%*	25.6%	480,388	2,135,795	22.5%
Swedbank	21.2%*	25.5%*	414,214	1,237,364	33.5%
Sydbank	13.9%*	16.0%*	72,467	152,316	47.6%
UBS	13.4%	18.9%	216,462	1,038,836	20.8%
UniCredit	10.0%	13.6%*	409,223	844,217	48.5%
UBI Unione di Banche	12.3%*	15.3%*	61,763	121,787	50.7%

Notes on the table:

- Banca Monte dei Paschi has target ratios for solvency ratio and CET 1 ratio of 10.9% and 10.2%, as set by supervisory authorities (Annual report 2014, p. 23).

- Danske Bank is designated as a SIFI (systemically important financial institution) in Denmark and was required to have an additional CET 1 ratio of 0.6% in 2015, increasing to 3% in 2019 (Annual report 2014, p. 39).

The data in the table gives us different answers about the banks analysed. The first column shows the CET 1 ratios and all banks are over the supervisory minimums. The absolute level of the ratio shows the solidity of a bank. The highest values are reached by Swiss and Scandinavian banks, both because of their special supervisory rules. The average CET 1 ratio is 12.7%. Compared to this, some Italian banks especially have very low CET 1 ratios, for example Banca Carige with 8.4%.

The CET 1 ratio has to be viewed in combination with the earnings situation of the bank. A low CET 1 ratio combined with a stable, high earnings situation is still sufficient. A low CET 1 ratio combined with an unstable or low earnings situation is very risky. Unfortunately, for the most part the unprofitable banks in this sample have low CET 1 ratios as well. Of all banks with a single digit CET 1 ratio, only Banco Santander and Bank of Ireland have a positive RoRWA, while the banks with the highest CET 1 ratios also have a very high RoRWA.

The following table shows the CET 1 ratio along with the RoRWA for the banks mentioned in this book.

Name	CET 1 ratio	RoRWA
Banca Carige	8.4%*	−2.67%
Banca Monte dei Paschi	8.7%*	−6.89%
Banco Bilbao Vizcaya Argentaria (BBVA)	10.4%	0.59%
Banco Comercial Portugues	8.9%	−0.79%
Banco de Sabadell	11.7%*	−1.82%

Name	CET 1 ratio	RoRWA
Banco Popolare	11.9%*	−4.34%
Banco Popular	11.5%*	0.41%
Banco Santander	9.7%	0.81%
Bank of Ireland	9.3%	0.64%
Bankia	12.3%*	0.76%
Bankinter	11.9%*	1.00%
Barclays	10.3%	0.25%
Banca Popolare di Sondrio	9.8%*	−0.26%
Banca Popolare del´Emilia Romagna	11.3%*	−0.61%
BNP Paribas	10.3%	0.73%
Caixabank	13.1%*	0.33%
Commerzbank	11.7%*	−0.10%
Credit Suisse	17.1%*	0.03%
Crédit Agricole	13.1%	0.67%
Danske Bank	15.1%*	1.26%
Deutsche Bank	11.7%	0.02%
DNB	12.7%*	1.70%
Erste Group Bank	10.6%*	0.48%
HSBC	11.1%	0.80%
Intesa Sanpaolo	13.5%*	−0.10%
Julius Bär	22.0%*	1.85%
Jyske Bank	15.3%*	0.06%
KBC	14.3%	0.92%
Komercni Banka	16.4%*	3.19%
Lloyds	12.8%*	0.76%
Mediobanca	12.0%*	0.21%

Name	CET 1 ratio	RoRWA
National Bank of Greece	13.6%*	0.18%
Natixis	11.4%*	0.48%
Nordea Bank	15.7%*	1.30%
Raiffeisen	10.9%	−0.34%
Royal Bank of Scotland	11.2%*	0.16%
SEB	16.3%*	2.43%
Société Générale	10.1%*	0.41%
Standard Chartered	10.7%	0.88%
Svenska Handelsbanken	20.4%*	3.09%
Swedbank	21.2%*	3.34%
Sydbank	13.9%*	1.40%
UBS	13.4%	0.58%
UniCredit	10.0%	0.21%
UBI Unione di Banche	12.3%*	−0.43%

The result of plotting the data is shown in the following chart.

We find only a few banks with a 2% RoRWA and a CET 1 ratio of more than 15% (right-hand side in the chart). These are the stars in the sample; very solid from the CET 1 ratio and highly profitable. In these group we find: Komercni Banka, SEB, Svenska Handelsbanken and Swedbank.

The second group (upper middle of the chart) contains solid banks (CET 1 ratio of more than 15%), but with problems on the earnings side (less than 2% RoRWA). In this group we find: Danske Bank, Julius Bär, Nordea Bank as the stronger banks (high RoRWA), and Credit Suisse and Jyske Bank as the weaker banks (low RoRWA).

The third group (left of the chart) contains weak banks with low CET 1 ratios and which are strongly unprofitable. This group contains: Banca Carige, Banca Monte dei Paschi, Banco Comercial Portugues, Banco de Sabadell and Banco Popolare. These banks are highly in danger.

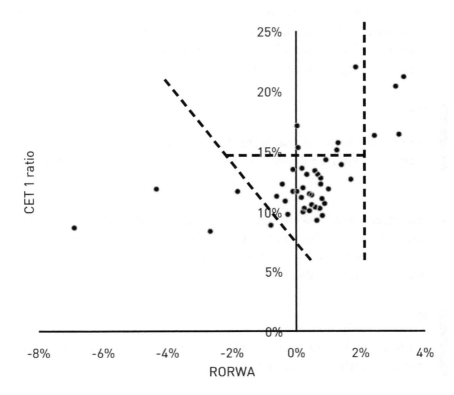

The remaining banks – containing the most banks used in this sample – are in the remaining big group (lower middle of the chart). These banks are lightly profitable or unprofitable with a lower CET 1 ratio. These banks are actually not in danger, but even small problems could lead to a dangerous position for these banks. They have problems on both the earnings side and the equity side.

In the first of the two tables, the quotient between risk-weighted assets and total assets is shown in the last column. It can show us the following:

- Whether the leverage ratio or CET 1 rate is decisive for a bank. Most banks have a value higher than 30% for the RWA/total assets and for these banks the CET 1 rate is the important one. For the other banks that have a value of less than 30% for RWA/total assets, the leverage is decisive. With Deutsche Bank and Natixis, two primarily investment banks which have the lowest values for RWA/ total assets, they are dependent on the leverage ratio. Both these two banks have low CET 1 rates so they have even bigger problems with meeting the leverage ratio.

Note

A low ratio between risk-weighted assets and total assets combined with a low CET 1 rate shows problems with the leverage ratio.

- The quotient of risk-weighted assets and total assets tells us about the riskiness of the bank. The higher the quotient, the higher the credit risks of the bank. Mostly Italian banks with high credit risks have high quotients here.

Note

A high (low) ratio between risk-weighted assets and total assets means usually high (low) risks.

- Last but not least, the quotient of risk-weighted assets and total assets has an effect on the meaning of the CET 1 ratio. A high CET 1 ratio combined with a low quotient is not that good because the leverage ratio will be much lower compared to the supervisory border than the CET 1 ratio. For example, Svenska Handelsbanken has a very high CET 1 ratio but a very low quotient. Its leverage ratio will be much lower compared to the supervisory border than the CET 1 ratio. The high average CET 1 ratio of Scandinavian banks is given another perspective by including the quotient in the analysis. The Scandinavian banks are very well capitalised, but this is mostly because of low risk calculated through risk-weighted assets than by high capital. A worse situation is when the CET 1 ratio is quite low with a low quotient, like Deutsche Bank or Natixis. These banks have to lower their total assets, not their risk-weighted assets, to have a buffer to the supervisory border.

Note

If the quotient of risk-weighted assets and total assets is too low and therefore the leverage ratio is a problem for a bank, it has to reduce its total assets and not its risk-weighted assets. The strategy has to be to reduce risk-free assets for the banking supervision rules – like treasuries – and not to reduce high-risk investments.

8. Stock Analysis

The stock exchange trades based on future income while the analyst is looking at income statements from the past. Under these circumstances, stock analysis always has to be viewed very carefully. But, as mentioned in chapter 2, bank profits are much more constant than non-bank profits. Following this point of view, even with the income statements from 2014 we can make a stock analysis.

In the following table the income after taxes is converted into euros for all banks. The following exchange rates were used where required:

- 1.28 GBP/€
- 1.2023 CHF/€
- 7.4468 DKK/€
- 0.11042 €/NOK
- 0.82638 €/US-$
- 0.03607 €/CZK
- 0.10560 €/SEK

Additionally, the price-earnings ratio (PER) for all banks (market capitalisation / income after taxes) is given.

Name	Home country	Market cap. (02.10.2015) in Bio. €	Market cap. rank	Income after taxes	PER
Banca Carige	Italy	1.2	45	−408	Neg.
Banca Monte dei Paschi	Italy	4.8	36	−5,254	Neg.
Banco Bilbao Vizcaya Argentaria (BBVA)	Spain	46.3	8	3,753	12.3
Banco Comercial Portugues	Portugal	3.1	41	−335	Neg.
Banco de Sabadell	Spain	8.6	30	770	11.2
Banco Popolare	Italy	4.7	37	−2,085	Neg.
Banco Popular	Spain	7.0	33	330	21.2
Banco Santander	Spain	65.8	3	4,748	13.9
Bank of Ireland	Ireland	11.2	27	330	33.9
Bankia	Spain	13.3	25	677	19.6
Bankinter	Spain	5.9	34	256	23.0
Barclays	UK	55.4	6	1,312	42.2
Banca Popolare di Sondrio	Italy	1.8	43	−55	Neg.
Banca Popolare dell'Emilia Romagna	Italy	3.6	39	−248	Neg.
BNP Paribas	France	64.7	4	4,525	14.3
Caixabank	Spain	20.1	22	1,071	18.8
Commerzbank	Germany	11.8	26	−205	Neg.
Credit Suisse	Switz.	34.5	10	76	453.9
Crédit Agricole	France	26.6	16	3,304	8.1

Name	Home country	Market cap. (02.10.2015) in Bio. €	Market cap. rank	Income after taxes	PER
Danske Bank	Denmark	27.2	15	1,469	18.5
Deutsche Bank	Germany	32.8	12	–94	Neg.
DNB	Norway	19.3	23	2,279	8.5
Erste Group Bank	Austria	11.0	28	–485	Neg.
HSBC	UK	134.3	1	8,072	16.6
Intesa Sanpaolo	Italy	48.8	7	–257	Neg.
Julius Bär	Switz.	9.4	29	305	30.8
Jyske Bank	Denmark	4.7	37	12	391.7
KBC	Belgium	23.5	18	839	28.0
Komercni Banka	Czech Republic	7.5	31	442	17.0
Lloyds	UK	73.9	2	2,321	31.8
Mediobanca	Italy	7.5	31	124	60.5
National Bank of Greece	Greece	1.3	44	107	12.1
Natixis	France	15,5	24	552	28.1
Nordea Bank	Sweden	41.4	9	2,896	14.3
Raiffeisen	Austria	3.4	40	–235	Neg.
Royal Bank of Scotland	UK	27.6	14	728	37.9
SEB	Sweden	20.9	21	1,584	13.2
Société Générale	France	31.9	13	1,448	22.0
Standard Chartered	UK	23.0	19	2,496	9.2
Svenska Handelsbanken	Sweden	23.9	17	1,565	15.3

Name	Home country	Market cap. (02.10.2015) in Bio. €	Market cap. rank	Income after taxes	PER
Swedbank	Sweden	22.5	20	1,488	15.1
Sydbank	Denmark	2.5	42	136	18.4
UBS	Switz.	61.0	5	1,539	39.6
UniCredit	Italy	33.2	11	873	38.0
UBI Unione di Banche	Italy	5.8	35	−265	Neg.

We can see that most of the banks have high numbers for the PER, many with a figure over 20. This says that banks still trade with very high prices on the stock exchange. The whole Stoxx 600 Banks has a PER of 26. Compared with the PER based on net income in the income statements, not corrected by extraordinary income, this PER is much higher than it should be.

Why do investors pay so much for banks?

When we look at the balance sheet of an industrial company, the equity there is only the residual value. When the company tries to sell its assets, most will not be sold at the value in the balance sheet, but much lower. The liquidation value of an industrial company will be much lower than the equity shown in the balance sheet.

In contrast to that, if a bank tries to sell its assets, the values in the balance sheet should be received by the bank because most of the values are from market prices. It may need some time to sell all the loans, securities and so on, but in fact most of the equity shown in the balance sheet will be regained by the shareholders.

Why then do some banks have a stock price far under the equity per share in the balance sheet?

First, investors assume that banks have higher risks than shown in the balance sheet, such as for provisions (see section 3.2). Second, banks are too important for the economy and cannot be allowed to go bankrupt, so investors look for earnings and many banks do not get sufficiently high returns on equity to get higher stock prices. Third, in many balance sheets there is goodwill and other intangible assets which investors assume are not worth the amount in the balance sheet.

In the following table, the market capitalisation, the equity on 31.12.2014 and the PER are included.

Name	Home country	Market cap. (02.10.2015) in Bio. €	Equity	PER
Banca Carige	Italy	1.2	2.9	Neg.
Banca Monte dei Paschi	Italy	4.8	6.0	Neg.
Banco Bilbao Vizcaya Argentaria (BBVA)	Spain	46.3	41.3	12.3
Banco Comercial Portugues	Portugal	3.1	4.2	Neg.
Banco de Sabadell	Spain	8.6	10.2	11.2
Banco Popolare	Italy	4.7	8,1	Neg.
Banco Popular	Spain	7.0	12.2	21.2
Banco Santander	Spain	65.8	51.8	13.9
Bank of Ireland	Ireland	11.2	8.8	33.9
Bankia	Spain	13.3	12.5	19.6
Bankinter	Spain	5.9	3.6	23.0
Barclays	UK	55.4	84.0	42.2
Banca Popolare di Sondrio	Italy	1.8	2.0	Neg.
Banca Popolare dell'Emilia Romagna	Italy	3.6	5.5	Neg.
BNP Paribas	France	64.7	57.2	14.3
Caixabank	Spain	20.1	25.2	18.8
Commerzbank	Germany	11.8	26.1	Neg.
Credit Suisse	Switzerland	34.5	36.6	453.9
Crédit Agricole	France	26.6	92.6	8.1

Name	Home country	Market cap. (02.10.2015) in Bio. €	Equity	PER
Danske Bank	Denmark	27.2	20.6	18.5
Deutsche Bank	Germany	32.8	68.4	Neg.
DNB	Norway	19.3	17.5	8.5
Erste Group Bank	Austria	11.0	13.4	Neg.
HSBC	UK	134.3	165.3	16.6
Intesa Sanpaolo	Italy	48.8	45.1	Neg.
Julius Bär	Switzerland	9.4	4.4	30.8
Jyske Bank	Denmark	4.7	3.7	391.7
KBC	Belgium	23.5	14.2	28.0
Komercni Banka	Czech Republic	7.5	3.8	17.0
Lloyds	UK	73.9	62.3	31.8
Mediobanca	Italy	7.5	8.8	60.5
National Bank of Greece	Greece	1.3	9.6	12.1
Natixis	France	15.5	18.9	28.1
Nordea Bank	Sweden	41.4	29.8	14.3
Raiffeisen	Austria	3.4	7.8	Neg.
Royal Bank of Scotland	UK	27.6	73.3	37.9
SEB	Sweden	20.9	14.2	13.2
Société Générale	France	31.9	55.2	22.0
Standard Chartered	UK	23.0	38.4	9.2
Svenska Handelsbanken	Sweden	23.9	13.4	15.3
Swedbank	Sweden	22.5	12.4	15.1
Sydbank	Denmark	2.5	1.5	18.4
UBS	Switzerland	61.0	44.9	39.6

Name	Home country	Market cap. (02.10.2015) in Bio. €	Equity	PER
UniCredit	Italy	33.2	52.8	38.0
UBI Unione di Banche	Italy	5.8	9.8	Neg.

First, many banks have a market capitalisation that is below the amount of equity in the balance sheet. This is the case for nearly all banks with a negative PER, but even for some profitable banks the market capitalisation is less than their equity.

In the next table, RoRWA and the ratio between market capitalisation and equity are shown.

Bank	RoRWA	Market capitalisation / equity
Banca Carige	−2.67%	41.4%
Banca Monte dei Paschi	−6.89%	80.0%
Banco Bilbao Vizcaya Argentaria (BBVA)	0.59%	112.1%
Banco Comercial Portugues	−0.79%	73.8%
Banco de Sabadell	−1.82%	84.3%
Banco Popolare	−4.34%	58.0%
Banco Popular	0.41%	57.4%
Banco Santander	0.81%	127.0%
Bank of Ireland	0.64%	127.3%
Bankia	0.76%	106.4%
Bankinter	1.00%	163.9%
Barclays	0.25%	66.0%
Banca Popolare di Sondrio	−0.26%	90.0%
Banca Popolare dell'Emilia Romagna	−0.61%	65.5%

Bank	RoRWA	Market capitalisation / equity
BNP Paribas	0.73%	113.1%
Caixabank	0.33%	79.8%
Commerzbank	−0.10%	45.2%
Credit Suisse	0.03%	94.3%
Crédit Agricole	0.67%	28.7%
Danske Bank	1.26%	132.0%
Deutsche Bank	0.02%	48.0%
DNB	1.70%	110.3%
Erste Group Bank	0.48%	82.1%
HSBC	0.80%	81.2%
Intesa Sanpaolo	−0.10%	108.2%
Julius Bär	1.85%	213.6%
Jyske Bank	0.06%	127.0%
KBC	0.92%	165.5%
Komercni Banka	3.19%	197.4%
Lloyds	0.76%	118.6%
Mediobanca	0.21%	85.2%
National Bank of Greece	0.18%	13.5%
Natixis	0.48%	82.0%
Nordea Bank	1.30%	138.9%
Raiffeisen	−0.34%	43.6%
Royal Bank of Scotland	0.16%	37.7%
SEB	2.43%	147.2%
Société Générale	0.41%	57.8%
Standard Chartered	0.88%	59.9%

Bank	RoRWA	Market capitalisation / equity
Svenska Handelsbanken	3.09%	178.4%
Swedbank	3.34%	181.5%
Sydbank	1.40%	166.7%
UBS	0.58%	135.9%
UniCredit	0.21%	62.9%
UBI Unione di Banche	−0.43%	59.2%

We can see a strong connection between market capitalisation / equity and RoRWA. Most banks with a negative RoRWA have a market capitalisation / equity under 100% and all banks with a RoRWA over 1% have a market capitalisation / equity over 100%, so investors pay a higher price for banks with a high RoRWA.

9. Conclusion

This book, with examples of 45 European banks using IFRS, has showed how to analyse bank financial statements in a few easy steps:

1. A few positions in the balance sheet can show us if a bank uses accounting policy to look better than it is. If we find problems here, it would be a strong warning about the bank.

2. Segment data can show us what the bank management wants us to believe. If unexpected data is shown, we should be extremely careful about the bank.

3. Several key figures can show if there are abnormalities in bank financial statements.

4. The RoRWA is the key indicator to compare banks and to make a judgement about them.

5. The CET 1 ratio is the key indicator for the financial health of a bank.

6. RoRWA and the CET 1 ratio together show the strength of a bank.

7. The leverage ratio is relevant for analysis if the percentage of risk-weighted assets or corrected total assets is lower than the value that has been specified as a target for the bank.